How to

Hypnotize

Yourself…

Without

Losing Your Mind

How to

Hypnotize

Yourself...

Without

Losing Your Mind

A Self-hypnosis Training Program
For
Students and Educators

By

Wayne F. Perkins
Certified Clinical Hypnotherapist

Copyright © 1999 by Wayne F. Perkins

All rights reserved. No part of this book may be reproduced,
stored in a retrieval system, or transmitted by any means,
electronic, mechanical, photocopying, recording, or otherwise,
without written permission from the author.

ISBN 1-58500-355-7

About the Book

Achieve All Of Your Goals: Now!

Do You Want to Learn A System That Will Help You Now and In The Future?

Would You Enjoy Learning Your New System In The Privacy, Security And Safety Of Your Home?

Would You Appreciate A Book That Addresses Your Specific Goals?

Wayne F. Perkins, Certified Clinical Hypnotherapist, gives you all the tools necessary to learn and master Self-hypnosis.

You will become the Master of your own Mind!

Each Chapter contains easy instructions and exercises specifically designed for mastery of self-hypnosis.

How do you achieve all of your goals using self-hypnosis? Wayne F. Perkins, Clinical Hypnotherapist, teaches you not only the principles and theories of hypnosis but allows you to experiment with self-hypnosis before much of the theory is presented.

How To Hypnotize Yourself Without Losing Your Mind, is a combination textbook/workbook, that teaches you step by step how and when to give yourself suggestions and then how to apply them to help you achieve all of your personal goals.The Perkins Method of Self-hypnosis may be used to teach their clients how to administer and master self-hypnosis.

Unlike most self-hypnosis books that begin with hypnosis justification, history, and theory, Wayne allows you to experience meaningful hypnosis by Chapter 3. Finishing Chapter 11, the reader/student will have been presented the complete art of self-suggestion. The reader may hyperlink to the history, theory, or hypnosis resources chapters at any time during the instruction, but it is not necessary. The reader controls where and when meaningful goal achievement instruction will take place.

"My mission in life is to help you achieve your mission in life."--Wayne F. Perkins, Certified Clinical Hypnotherapist

Dedication

I dedicate this book to you, the reader and goal achiever. You are my inspiration.
I also dedicate this book to all of the people who have inspired me during my life. You continue to inspire me and you are helping others achieve their mission in life.

Wayne F. Perkins
Certified Clinical Hypnotherapist

"My mission in life is to help you achieve your mission in life."--Wayne F. Perkins

How to Use This Book

How To Hypnotize Yourself Without Losing Your Mind, by Wayne F. Perkins, is not just a book. It is a complete self-hypnosis-training program.

The Perkins Method of Self-hypnosis involves reading text, recording your text into a tape recorder, and then listening to the text on a regular basis. The authored text and your own creations of inductions and hypnotic prescriptions or prevailing thoughts, guarantee your personal goal achievement.

Not only do you receive self-hypnosis in its classic sense, but also powerful goal achievement techniques created by Wayne F. Perkins, and other top sales trainers throughout the United States.

In addition to reading and recording the text presented in this portion of the program, you have access to powerful Internet resources. These resources include a Self-hypnosis Chat service that provides on-line and real-time answers to your personal challenges. Other hypnotherapists and students with similar challenges discuss answers with the reader.

The Self-hypnosis Forum located on the Internet provides similar help. A major advantage in using this resource is that messages may be read and posted 24 hours a day. This is a great advantage to the many students from countries that participate.

Updated Chapters to this book and the Appendices are available to registered users of this book. A site on the Internet will provide free updated information and new Chapters. You and your program, *How To Hypnotize Yourself Without Losing Your Mind,* are a work in progress. New insights and pages will be added without additional cost to you. Since the new information is located on the Internet, it will be easy to copy and print out for your use.

Advantages for Hypnotherapists and Hypnosis Educators

How To Hypnotize Yourself Without Losing Your Mind is a powerful textbook/workbook for your students. It provides a step by step approach to teaching self-hypnosis that guarantees positive results for your students. The book is filled with activities for the students. It allows you to integrate your personal beliefs and systems for best results for your students and their goals.

The Perkins Self-hypnosis Method, using Internet resources, is studied by students and educators located in: Australia, Belgium, Canada, England, Egypt, India, Ireland, Japan, Jordan, Malaysia, Nepal, Nevis, South Africa, and Switzerland, as well as in the United States.

Contents

Part 1

How to Hypnotize Yourself

Self-hypnosis Training

Chapter 1 What Is Self-Hypnosis? How Can It Help?

Introduction

Would you like to achieve all of your goals in life? Would you like to accomplish this task the "easy" way?

My name is Wayne Perkins and I have been an Educational Hypnotist and Clinical Hypnotherapist for over 20 years. I have helped many people achieve their goals in life. I have taught them how to accomplish this task the "easy" way. People have mastered the art of self-hypnosis.

What is self-hypnosis?

Self-hypnosis refers to the power that words and ideas have when we surround these words and ideas with our complete attention. A hypnotist or an operator delivers words and ideas. However, you may write them down, all by yourself. You may record and deliver those words and ideas to your powerful subconscious mind. When you change the words and ideas you have swimming around in your head from negative words and conditions to positive words and conditions, many wonderful things happen.

The best thing that happens is that you realize the goal or behavior that you have been concentrating on. This goal may include losing a specific amount of weight. Your goal may be to sleep better at night. You may want to relax better during stressful periods during the day. Any and all goals that you are trying to accomplish in life may be accomplished through the use of self-hypnosis and powerful goal setting techniques.

Part 1 of *How To Hypnotize Yourself Without Losing Your Mind,* includes Chapters 1-11. You will be reading, recording, and practicing many self-hypnosis and goals setting techniques.

Part 2 of *How To Hypnotize Yourself Without Losing Your Mind,* includes Chapters 14,15, and the appendices. Part 2 includes hypnosis definitions and theory, the history of hypnosis, reference books on hypnosis, and hypnosis and goal achievement resources located on the Internet.

Feel free at any time to turn to Chapter 14 to learn more about the theory when you feel it appropriate or use any of the resources when you need them.

This book does not have to be read cover to cover for you to achieve success. In fact by the end of the third chapter, you will have already achieved success!

My mission in life is to help you achieve your mission in life. The major tools I use to guarantee your success in achieving your mission are self-hypnosis techniques. These techniques you learn and master. You then apply them for to all of your goals in life.

When you have questions regarding hypnosis and self-hypnosis as you read this book, please visit the Internet resources located in the appendix or my Hypnotism Education Website located at:

http://www.wayneperkins.net

The Self-hypnosis Forum located at the Hypnotism Education Website will also provide you with help regarding self-hypnosis and its applications. You will find the information you need. You may also send me e-mail at:

wayne@wayneperkins.net

You will also find support groups on-line that will guarantee the success of all of your goals in life. Support groups information and Internet hyperlinks are found in Appendix D.

If you do not have Internet access, I would strongly recommend that you get access. Rapidly, there are becoming two major classes of people in the world. There are the information rich and the information poor. You get to choose which class you will belong. Make sure you are in the information rich and you will receive all the information you need regarding help in any area you can imagine. Most of this valuable information will cost you nothing.

You get to choose which class you will belong. Which one do you choose?

How Can Self-hypnosis Help?

Here is how self-hypnosis can help.

1. Just by the act of relaxing, you will find peace and harmony on your way to goal achievement.
2. By focussing on specific thoughts and ideas when in the state of self-hypnosis your powerful subconscious mind will act on your goals in a most profound manner.

Each chapter will contain exercise both written and recorded that will focus on the act of relaxing and upon your specific thoughts and ideas constructed to help you achieve your specific goals. Activities assigned at the end of each chapter will target your specific goals and help you achieve them quickly.

What To Expect From Me

My mission in life is to help you achieve your mission in life. The way I will help you achieve your mission in life is to teach you self-hypnosis and powerful goal achieving techniques, specifically designed for your success.

You can expect from me all that I have and all that I can give in helping you achieve your goals. This book contains a plethora of information in the appendices that will insure your success. Once you send me your registration form located in Appendix A-1 in this book, you will receive help additional from my Internet site, Hypnotism Education Website located at:

http://www.wayneperkins.net

In addition to the information available to everyone who enters my website, registered book users will receive a private location on the site where you will find updated versions of each chapter of this book. You will also find additional pages and new chapters for this book. Life is a work in progress. Your life and my life is a work in progress. Hypnosis and self-hypnosis is a work in progress. As I find new discoveries in self-hypnosis, instead of forcing you to buy a second or third reprint, you will have access to the additional pages at my Internet address.

Just as you will grow in life, so will your self-hypnosis-training program.

Your *How To Hypnotize Yourself Without Losing Your Mind,* self-hypnosis training program will be updated and available for you for with no additional expense to you.

Pictures of my classes and me are available at the private Internet address for registered users.

You will also find in the appendix, offers for free attendance at my Self-hypnosis Training Workshops, called How To Hypnotize Yourself Without Losing Your Mind. You will receive discounts on other workshops and seminars I offer as well as discounts through my Hypnosis Bookstore located on the Internet at:

http://www.wayneperkins.net/hypnosis/books.html

Lists of many support groups that you may look upon for help are also listed in the appendices. I expect to give you my best to insure your success in life.

What To Expect From Yourself

Each Chapter has a specific purpose. By completing and applying Chapter's 1-11, you will be well on your way to goal achieving success. In fact, shortly after Chapter 4, you may have already attained the goal that was the purpose of you purchasing this book in the first place!

Many self-hypnosis books on the market are designed to be read from cover to cover. I have a problem with that.

Surveys show that self-improvement books are purchased, but rarely read cover to cover, like a novel. Self-hypnosis books begin with examples of self-hypnosis success, history, theory and then finally the self-hypnosis induction.

I have purposely designed this book so you will achieve success in your goals, long before you have read all of the theory or history. At any time you may skip to Part 2 where theory and history are located, but they are not necessary for your success.

If you read and perform the "Activities" in Chapters 1-11, you will have achieved a great deal of success.

Be sure to perform all of the activities. Although you may achieve all of the success you can ever imagine without doing everything, you will be exposed to many ways of achieving goals that will be sound information to use while instructing others how to achieve their goals. Part of the activities will be centered on you helping others. As you help others you will help yourself. When you achieve your goals, others will be inspired.

Always expect the best for yourself during your reading and completing of the assigned activities. Up until now, you may not have always expected the best for yourself and others. You must change that expectation if you wish to succeed at all you wish to accomplish in life. Wish success for yourself and wish success for others. Project success and happiness on all of your friends and on all of your enemies as well. As you focus on these thoughts, you will find your list of friends growing and your list of enemies shrinking. Always **expect** the best and you will **receive** the best.

Fundamental Law of Attraction

A fundamental law of attraction as it applies to self-hypnosis is as follows:

Whatever you hold in your mind at any given time, your body moves toward that direction.

Think about eating your favorite food. Picture in your mind how wonderful it looks. Picture in your mind the color and texture of the food. Think about how it feels as you chew it. Think about how your favorite food tastes and smells. Feel it in your mouth. Notice how your mouth starts to fill with saliva as you think these thoughts. This is the law of attraction at work. You are holding the thoughts of your favorite food in your mind. As you think about it in great detail your body tends to move toward it by allowing the saliva to flow as if you are digesting the food in real life. Do you begin to salivate when walking by a bakery or in a movie theater when you smell the popcorn popping? Notice how your body seems to be goal oriented. We will capitalize on that goal orientation of the body and the law of attraction as we progress through the self-hypnosis exercises. Remember that more theory will be discussed in Chapter 14. You may wish to read that now or wait until later. You get to make that choice.

Shortly, I will have you list those goals you wish to accomplish with your self-hypnosis program. Remember that as you list these goals on a piece of paper you will already start your subconscious mind on the road to completing those goals.

I am committed in helping you achieve success. Your job is to relax, follow my directions, and enjoy the process. Enjoy the book and the entire program!

Who Is This Book For?

This book has been specifically designed for you! Along with you, *How To Hypnotize Yourself Without Losing Your Mind* is designed for the following groups:

Students, parents, teachers, hypnotists, hypnotherapists, researchers, athletes, men, women, managers, workers, people with life-challenging illnesses, people that are perfectly healthy, in other words, **everyone**.

If you are a hypnotherapist looking for an easy to read and understand self-hypnosis learning system, this program will be a good choice. My website and all of the features at *The Hypnotism Education Website* will support you and your students in their journey of understanding and mastering self-hypnosis. You will be able to maintain control and add your own personal beliefs and theories. Registered users of this book are encouraged to send me their success stories as well as theories to add to the "book on demand" advantage. You will find that as you help others from around the world, you will help yourself.

The only way to effectively learn self-hypnosis is to for you to experience self-hypnosis. We will be experiencing self-hypnosis in future lessons. We will be doing that a lot!

What Do You Wish To Achieve?

Do you want to learn self-hypnosis because it sounds interesting?

Do you want to learn it to become master of your mind and master of your destiny?

Do you want to learn self-hypnosis to improve your relations with others?

Do you want to learn self-hypnosis to overcome Test Anxiety or improve in your studies?

Do you want to learn how to sleep better at night?

Do you want to learn how to overcome weight or smoking problems?

Do you want to improve in sports performance?

Do you want to be more creative?

Do you want to become more intuitive?

You may accomplish any or all of the above goals just by following the easy instructions in this learning system.

Workshop

Activity 1- What Are Your Goals?

List below 5 goals you wish to achieve.
1.

2.

3.

4.

5.

Activity 2 - What Will I Gain or Lose?

Think about this question: What will I gain by achieving this goal? Think about how your goal achievement will change your life. Also list all of the things you may lose as a result of your goals achievement. For example, if you are trying to control your weight, you will *lose* fat and you may also lose friends who would rather see you in the fat state you are in. For some reason they may feel that your success in weight control, diminishes them in some way. I am sure in your life experiences you have similar examples on how friends and relative really perceive you and support you in your success.

What will I gain by achieving my listed goals?
1.

2.

3.

4.

5.

What I will lose by achieving my listed goals?
1.

2.

3.

4.

5.

Keep the above list handy and feel free to read it over as we progress through the book. If you need more space to write, reproduce the extra forms located in Appendix B.

Activity 3 - Using The Self-hypnosis Forum For My Success

If you have an Internet provider dial up to your account and enter the following link into your browser.

http://www.wayneperkins.net

From there, click on the link that is marked, "Hypnosis Forum." There you will need to enter in your e-mail address and then proceed to the Forum. Read the "posts" there and feel free to participate, as you feel necessary. You may find a new support group just by participating at the Self-hypnosis Forum."

Summary

In Chapter 1, you learned that self-hypnosis involves the power that words and ideas have when surrounded by your complete attention.

A hypnotist may deliver the ideas or you may deliver the ideas to yourself.

You accomplish your goals by writing them down on a piece of paper, recording the ideas on tape and listening to them while in a relaxed state.

You learned that Part 2 of this book includes hypnosis theory and history in case you require more detail and clarification.

You learned that self-hypnosis can help you by relaxing you and by focusing on powerful goal oriented ideas and thoughts.

I am committed in helping you achieve success. Your job is to relax, follow my directions, and enjoy the process. Enjoy your self-hypnosis learning system!

Chapter 2 What Is Hypnosis?
Andrew

Four people volunteered to be my hypnotic subjects. Two men and two women were listening to each and every word I was saying. I asked that they rise up from their chairs and "step forward, walking and sleeping, walking and sleeping." Out of the four subjects, only one, a woman, stepped forward and obeyed my command. The others opened their eyes, aroused themselves from any hypnosis influence I had on them, and listened and watched me as I worked with the sleepwalking woman. I suggested that when the woman's eyes open, her arms would be stuck in front of her and she would not remember her name, until I snap my fingers beside her ear. She responded to those suggestions and the other people watching told me they were impressed.

This was my first attempt at hypnotizing other people.

The next day, which was Saturday, I received a phone call from Andrew. He was one of the three volunteers who were not responsive to my hypnotic induction, the night before. I will always refer to him in this book as Andrew. Andrew was appreciative of my efforts the night before. He thanked me over and over and apologized for not responding well, not "going under the hypnotic spell." I had no idea both of our lives would now change, forever.

Andrew explained to me on the telephone, that he needed to see me right away. He begged me to come to his home. He would clarify everything when I arrived. When he met me at the door he looked very nervous and upset. He was always such a happy, calm and confident man, I knew what he had to say was very important.

Andrew admitted that he suffered from acrophobia, a severe fear of heights. But it wasn't an ordinary "fear of heights," that required him to contact me. Andrew's fear was so intense, he could not ride on an elevator or walk up the stairs of a second story building! If the building had windows facing outside, Andrew would not enter. I said I wasn't a psychologist or psychiatrist and suggested that he find one to help him overcome his fear. He had no time to explore this option because in a few hours, two friends were coming over to have him his first ride in an airplane to help him overcome this fear.

Can you imagine the intense fear Andrew must have had at the time? Can you feel yourself in his place, knowing you would leave the ground in a small aircraft without the benefit of a solid support beneath your feet? This was his first time up in an airplane and it would be a very small aircraft. Andrew was paralyzed in fear.

After hearing his request, I wanted to help, but I remembered that Andrew was not responsive to my hypnotic commands the night before. I was not successful in putting him "under."

After failing to achieve a deep hypnotic trance, or even a light hypnotic trance, would he now reject any helpful suggestions I would give him?

There was only one way to find out!

Andrew was a very likable person, with a beautiful wife and family. He was well respected in the community and was about to embark in raising himself to new levels in his career. His career was launching into space. Soon he would be in the clouds, rocketing to the stars.

I proceeded to use a progressive relaxation technique of hypnosis. Andrew was concentrating on relaxing all the major muscle groups in his body. At the same time, Andrew was narrowing his mental concentration down to one thought. How good it felt to relax in this way. I taught him self-hypnosis and gave him an exercise to perform while he was in the aircraft. This exercise is the same exercise I will give you later. This is called a hypnotic "prescription, or prevailing thought."

The doorbell rang and Andrew's pilot buddies were at the door. We all went to the small rural airport. There, I told

Andrew I would stay on the ground and observe. He would need to confront his fear by himself using the exercises I had given him just a few minutes before. Andrew and the two pilots got in the small aircraft. After a few moments the aircraft was in the air. As it lifted off the ground I wondered if Andrew would be okay. Was he using the exercises I gave him to relax and achieve his goal? Could he maintain the mental state necessary to get through this crisis? Would he hypnotize himself so hard he would lose his mind?

Even though the aircraft was in the air for about an hour, it seemed like days. My neck hurt from gazing up at the heavens for such a long period of time. The tension was unbearable. The aircraft landed. Three figures headed toward me. I felt it was a good sign to see Andrew walking under his own power. He looked okay and finally said, "Wayne, that wasn't so bad."

The following Wednesday morning he called my on the telephone to invite me to breakfast. There he began to tell me he was entering flight training. Andrew was going to get a pilot's license! A lifetime of fear is gone in a flash, because he used his imagination and mind power to control it. He was able to overcome a major hurdle on his road to success.

More importantly, he didn't lose his mind!

I am proud of Andrew! Just as I am going to be proud of you when you write, call or e-mail me, with your personal success story.

What is hypnotism?

Is hypnotism a trance? Is hypnosis, one person dominating another or creating a situation to embarrass another? Can you get stuck in hypnosis?

Andrew helped me understand the definition of hypnotism that I have embraced now for over 20 years. Hypnotism is the "power words have when surrounded by your complete attention." Hypnotism can also be looked at as "the narrowing of our concentration down to just one or two core thoughts." How we get the·subject to narrow concentration down to just one or two core thoughts. We ask the subject think of nothing but peaceful and relaxing thoughts.

Mike Hayashi, a martial arts instructor and from Phoenix, Arizona, teaches the acronym for the word fear is: false expectations appearing real. Do you have false expectations appearing real? Does everyone have some fear or phobia that is holding them back from top achievement? Are you ready to change false expectations into positive expectations? Let's do it together! I will be with you every step of the way. Even when you feel no one is supporting you in your journey, remember that I will. My words will go with you, wherever and whenever you may need them.

In Chapter 1 we explored what self-hypnosis was and how it would help you. Review the assignment at the end of Chapter 1. Did you find it difficult? Did it make you think? Hypnosis and self-hypnosis techniques are designed to make you think and communicate with your powerful subconscious mind. They are designed to allow you to think from another perspective. They allow you to think very honestly about your personal situation.

In Chapter 2, we will learn more about to expect from the reality of hypnosis and self-hypnosis and will begin our success plan starting with Chapter 3. From Chapter 3 until Chapter 12, we will be implementing and exercising your goal success plan. For now, we will clear up a few things about hypnosis.

What Is A Goal?

Caveat Robert, the founder of the National Speakers Association, used the following quote to illustrate the definition of a "goal," Caveat said: "a goal is a dream with a deadline." Think about it. Have you ever wanted something and placed a time limit on acquiring it? Just before the time expired, did you miraculously receive it? That is the power of a goal. Once you wrap all of your emotions, your thoughts and your resources around your goal, and combine it with a deadline, you are rapidly achieving your goal.

Why do I define "goals" before we define "hypnotism?" Because in order to be successful at self-hypnotism, you must understand that it is all about goals and goal setting. We are creating "dreams with deadlines," with each and every successful hypnotic induction.

Go back to your assignment for Chapter 1, and place dates beside your goals. Make the dates realistic or unrealistic. Either way your body will be moving toward making those goals and dreams come true. You are in complete control.

What Is Hypnotism, Stage Hypnotism, Self-hypnotism?

Hypnotism is the power that words have when surrounded by our complete attention.

Did you ever get *lost* in a book that was exciting to you? If someone talks to you while you are in this mental state of mind, do you hear or even care what he or she is saying? Did you ever listen to music that would bring to mind and incident that took place many years before? Was that incident so clear in your memory that you felt that you were reliving it? Did you ever fall in love?

If you answered "yes" to any of the above questions, you have experienced hypnotism.

Did you ever get stuck? Did you realize that if an emergency took place while you were in this state of mind that you would be able to respond to the emergency? The book touched your imagination in such a way that the words and ideas presented in the book were surrounded by your complete attention. The music touched your imagination in such a way that a very clear memory associated with the music caught your imagination and became the focus of your complete attention. When you fall in love, what happens? Is your imagination stimulated in a way that you overlook physical, mental and emotional characteristics that others, (usually friends, relatives, or the local law enforcement officials) bring to your attention?

If hypnotism sounds like nothing special or a very common state of mind, you are perfectly correct in your thinking. Using this state of mind to achieve your personal goals is why you are reading this book.

What Is Stage Hypnotism?

Stage hypnotism involves two or more persons working together to realize one person's goal. One person is the hypnotist or *operator*. The other person is the *subject* or *hypnotee*. The goal of the stage hypnotist is to entertain. The goal of the subject is to help the stage hypnotist achieve his goal. The stage hypnotist captures the subject's attention, then presents words and ideas in such a way that the subject's imagination is stimulated and the ideas are carried out. Remember that the subject must want the hypnotist's goals to materialize or they just won't happen.

Think about Andrew. Andrew did not respond to any of the stage hypnotism I performed. However, when the goal of overcoming the fear of heights was his goal, Andrew's motivation and desire helped him overcome his fear with the assistance of the same hypnotist as his operator.

Is The Stage Hypnotist All Powerful?

Some of these ideas, such as the hypnotee acting with a different personality, or becoming insensitive to pain will be carried out to the amazement of the audience. Sometimes people get the feeling that the hypnotist has a strange, super human power.

The stage hypnotist is not born with some type of strange power over people. The stage hypnotist is working with the basic definition of hypnotism and using psychological principles that we will explain and you will utilize and practice in future chapters. More theory is located in Chapter 14 and on the

Hypnotism Education Website located at:

http://www.wayneperkins.net

What Is Self-hypnotism?

Self-hypnotism involves presenting words and ideas to yourself in a way that will captivate your attention and move you to some type of action. You surround yourself with words and ideas meant to bring about a change. But instead of having the change for an hour or so on stage, the change is meant to last a lifetime.

For example, if you want to lose weight, you may present words and ideas to yourself that involve how wonderful you will look and feel after you lose the appropriate weight. You wish to look and feel wonderful today, tomorrow, and many years from now. You may see yourself in the future getting compliments from all of your friends and relatives and perhaps see yourself in new, exciting relationships or stimulating events.

In this book, you will be presenting many words and ideas to yourself. You will present them in a way that will guarantee your success in the challenges of your life now, and your life ahead.

How Can I Benefit By Using Self-hypnosis?

The following is a brief list of uses of self-hypnosis. Can you think of any more?

> Improve memory and recall
> Develop positive self-esteem
> Reduce stress
> Reduce or eliminate physical pain
> Develop deep relaxation techniques

Sleep better at night
Overcome the fear of failure
Overcome the fear of success
Overcome shyness
Lose weight
Stop smoking
Achieve more self-confidence
Improve sports performance
Improve motivation
Improve concentration and retention of information
Control smoking
Overcome sexual problems
Improve sexual performance
Improve your immune system
Lower blood pressure

The list is endless! I have personally worked with people, both as individuals and as groups to achieve these benefits of self-hypnosis. Think about challenges you have. Continue the list.

Feel free at any time to look at the free scripts or prescriptions located on my site, or you may want some of them delivered to you by my "deeply hypnotized robot." You may find them on the Internet at this location:

http://www.wayneperkins.net

Click on the link that says: **Free To You**. Other hypnosis scripts can be found on my Hypnotism Education Website. Additional scripts and support groups can be found in Appendix D of this book. Use everything you can to achieve your personal success.

How Does It Work?

You learn how to relax and open your mind toward self-hypnosis. As you learn to relax deeply on my command or request, a strange thing begins to happen. You begin to accept suggestions that will be of benefit to you. A suggestion is simply an idea or thought that is implanted into your subconscious mind and when teamed up with repetition, becomes reality. The body responds to the ideas or thoughts you put in your mind. After enough repetitions of these thoughts are received, the mind starts to reprogram itself to respond the way you want it to.

How many repetitions does it take? It's hard to make any assumptions. Some people will begin to change their behavior after the very first session. Most people need many repetitions to insure that the desired behavior will override the undesired behavior.

What Will You Learn To Do?

You will learn how to present yourself with words and ideas. You will surround these words and ideas with your complete attention. Then you learn how to word suggestions in a way to give you the best opportunity to affect your subconscious mind. Then I teach you to create hypnotic prescriptions that are personal to you and specific to overcome your challenges and achieve your goals. You will then give yourself these suggestions or ideas many, many times before you finish the book.

The good news is that repetition of these positive thoughts and ideas will eventually create your goal achievement.

You will succeed!

When Do You Start This Wonderful Journey?

You have already begun. The journey into your subconscious

began as you completed the assignment in Chapter 1. It will continue with Chapter 3 in which you will learn how to hypnotize yourself.

Workshop

Turn the page back to your completed exercises in Chapter 1. Remember the assignment you had for Chapter 1. Take the list of goals and compare them with the list of uses of self-hypnosis. How do they compare?

Activity 1 - Write down 5 new goals on your list

You should have a total of 10 including the assignment from Chapter 1.

1.
2.
3.
4.
5.
6.
7.
8.
9.
10.

Activity 2 - Recording your goals

Take out your cassette tape recorder or other voice-recording device. Begin with a fresh new tape and title it, *My Goals*. Record on the tape the goals you wish to work on in this class. If you have more than 10, that is fine.

Activity 3 - Listening to your voice

After you are finished recording, listen to your voice on the recording at least twice a day. You pick the best times for this exercise. The times you pick will be the right times.

Activity 4 - Participate in the Self-hypnosis Forum

Follow the link to the Self-hypnosis Forum located at:

http://www.wayneperkins.net

Has anyone posted his or her personal goals? How do they compare with yours?

When you are finished with the assignments you will be ready to experience your first hypnotic induction exercise.

Let's begin!

Summary

In Chapter 2, you learned a new definition of goals.

You learned to define hypnotism, stage hypnotism and self-hypnotism.

You now know the similarities and differences of each.

You also learned many uses for self-hypnosis

Chapter 3 Hypnotic Conditioning
Jim

I went over to Jim's house to hypnotize him to overcome test anxiety. I decided to use a standard induction followed by a quick instruction on self-hypnosis. Overcoming test anxiety was always an easy session. Since I would be travelling on the road for several weeks, I would not be able to return in time to give Jim another hypnotic induction for reinforcement.

I figured the quickest and easiest way to help Jim overcome test anxiety was to work with my 10-step self-hypnosis program. This program was very rigid and Jim would have to follow each direction in the specific order it was given.

Jim was out of school about 10 years and had a chance to become an air traffic controller if he could pass the rigorous test. As I entered his living room, I looked around for symbols that may represent success, achievement, relaxation or courage. I always like to use something personal in the client's home. This is the place where the self-hypnosis plan will be reinforced. I want the client to have all the tools he/she needs. As Jim sat on his couch readying himself for hypnosis, I noticed a painting on the living room wall. The painting was an image of a magnificent lion. I decided to use this image as a focal point for Jim as he practiced his self-hypnosis exercises. After hypnotizing Jim and then teaching him my 10-step method on *How to Hypnotize Yourself*, I assured him, that he would do well on his air traffic controller's test.

Just as I was at the door, leaving, Jim's wife came home and had a request for me. She asked if I could help Jim, quit smoking. I gave about 5 minutes worth of advice and hurried my way out of his house.

About six months later I was in a restaurant when Jim and his wife saw me and came over to my table. Jim was excited and related to me how he passed his test and now was an air traffic controller. His wife added that Jim had quit smoking. Jim excited explained to me how he used my 5-step program every day. (Do you remember I had a ten-step program?)

I was polite and just answered, "yes." He went on to explain the 5-step plan and explain how he uses the picture on the magnificent lion to give him the courage to survive in *the jungle*. I listened intently as he told me how he mastered these techniques and said he can't wait to develop more problems so that he hand handle them through his self-hypnosis program.

After Jim and his wife left, I thought hard about what he said. Jim stated he used a 5-step program not a 10-step like I had advised. Also, he didn't even use the 5 steps in the correct order I presented. What this demonstrates is that I want you to learn the principles as I teach them but remember that what you decide works for you, go for it. You are the best hypnotist in the world when it comes to your own problems. I can teach you to talk to your subconscious mind in a way that you will understand. I can perform a lot of exercises and hypnotic inductions, but all of the *healing* that goes on comes from you and you only.

This is exciting! You can take what I give you, personalize it, and make it work. You don't need to get bogged down in a lot of theory and worry about your technique. One of the main reasons I place the history and theory of hypnosis in the back of the book is to allow you to experiment and become successful without having to judge your own form and technique. You are going to become very successful at hypnotizing yourself. You are going to achieve all of your goals in life.

Before we begin with your first hypnotic induction performed by the greatest hypnotist in the world, I would like to go over some typical questions you may have in your mind, regarding self-hypnosis and hypnosis.

First of all, there is no button in your brain that you push to become hypnotized or dehypnotized. Becoming hypnotized is just following directions and concentrating so intently on a particular thought or string of thoughts, that nothing else that is going on around you seems to be distracting or very important.

Since there is no button to push, there is no button to get *stuck* and have you frozen in hypnosis or self-hypnosis. In all of the history of hypnotism, no one has ever gotten *stuck*. That's too bad, because it is a wonderful state of mind to be experiencing.

You will hear all the instructions given. Whether I am giving you instructions in person or you are giving them to yourself, you will hear everything that goes on around you and everything that the hypnotist is saying. The only time you won't hear everything that is being said is if you go to sleep. As you relax in hypnosis it is very easy to fall into natural sleep. In a few minutes, however, you will wake up on your own. You will, however, respond to any suggestion you gave yourself before falling into natural sleep.

When you listen to a hypnotist or your own hypnotic recording, do not evaluate or judge what is going on. There will be plenty of time to evaluate the process once you are back into the *waking state of mind*.

Your mind works better at accepting positive suggestions when your body is at rest and your mind is just listening to each and every word the hypnotist is saying. Listen to the words as you listened to parents when you were a child of five or six years of age. Remember that anything is possible when you are in the hypnotic state of mind.

Here are a list of FAQS or Frequently Asked Questions, regarding hypnosis and self-hypnosis. When you have additional questions feel free to visit my Hypnotism Education Website at:

http://www.wayneperkins.net

You will find additional FAQS on the Website as well as the Self-hypnosis Forum. You may want to join. People from around the world have the same questions as you regarding self-hypnosis. They will also share with you how they have overcome problems and achieved goals with self-hypnosis. Other hypnotherapists and health card professionals will share their experiences with you as well. Below are some FAQS, (frequently asked questions) which is pronounced "fax."

Question: Will I get stuck in hypnosis?

Answer: No, hypnosis is a state of concentration and consciousness not un-consciousness.

Question: Will I hear noises around me?

Answer: Yes, you will be aware of everything around you. You may, however, select to minimize other conversations or stimuli.

Question: How do I know when I am hypnotized?

Answer: You are conditioning yourself for hypnosis. Don't worry, just allow yourself to relax. All that is important are the results from hypnosis, not the process.

Question: What does it feel like?

Answer: It feels like whatever you want it to feel like. If you want to feel a tingling sensation all over your body, then that is what you will feel. If you want to feel warm or cold, you will feel warm or cold.

Question: Will I remember everything of the session?

Answer: You will remember everything. (Unless you fall asleep while practicing) Then you may remember only those suggestions given until you drifted off to sleep.

Question: How often should I practice self-hypnosis?

Answer: Practice it as often as you desire. Repetition helps you relax better each time. Repetition of positive suggestions even in the waking state will help you achieve your success achievement plan.

Question: Where can I find out more about the hypnotic condition?

Answer: Check out my FAQ's located on the Hypnosis Education Website, located at: http://www.wayneperkins.net Also I have provide a list of resources in Appendix D of this book.

Objectives of Chapter 3

The major objectives of Chapter 3 are to teach you how to give yourself an hypnotic induction, record it on tape, and listen to the induction with maximum results. Its sounds like a lot to expect at this part in the book. However, remember that the best hypnotist in the world for your success, is you. Once you have accepted that statement in your subconscious, you will be able to achieve results you never believed possible.

Instructions for Your Self-hypnosis Recording

Listen by yourself for the first few sessions. Do not tell anyone that you are going to work on a problem with self-hypnosis. Other people's views and misconceptions of hypnosis will come into play if others are brought in to the process at this phase. Let yourself have many positive experiences with self-hypnosis to share with your friends at a later date. Your success is the most important issue here, not the validation of your friends.

Remember that since your mind will be very alert during this exercise, you will be able to react to any emergency that is going on around you.

Practice this skill over and over. Repetition will help condition you faster.

As you read the following script into your recording equipment, read in a slow, relaxed style. As you are reading the script into your recording device, you may notice how I say things like, "you are going deep asleep, or you will feel alive and alert." Record this exercise first exactly as written and then substitute, the word, "I' for you. Practice and see, which exercise you, enjoy best.

Use a new tape for each new induction. Label each tape to correspond with each Chapter. This is Chapter 3, Self-hypnosis Conditioning, Eyes Open Method. Side B of the tape may be labeled Eyes Open Method with "I."

If you fall asleep during the exercise, don't worry. Practice sitting in a less comfortable chair next time. You were probably just a little too relaxed as you lay on your bed.

As you read the hypnosis conditioning script into your recorder, pause for 3 seconds each time you see the (Pause) cue.

Self-hypnosis Induction 1: Eyes Open Method

Always remember that ALL hypnosis is self-hypnosis! You are always in control. You have all the power necessary to make positive changes in your own life. You may have found out already in life that you also have the power to make all the negative changes in your life. Let's focus on the positive changes.

Find an area in your home or place of work where you can have about 10 minutes to yourself. That's right, only 10 minutes are needed in your quest for a successful induction at this point. After practicing this exercise many times, you may reduce the time to only one or two minutes. Now read the following words into a recording device. Read very, very slowly. Pretend that you are tired as you read this exercise and you will react in a relaxed, sleepy, manner. You will find yourself empathetic to your own voice. You may want to print out this page for future reference. Whenever you see the (Pause) cue, pause for 3 seconds, then go ahead and read again. Let your body relax for a few moments before continuing to record.

BEGINNING OF EXERCISE

Sit up in a comfortable chair or lie on a couch or a bed with your hands resting in your lap or by your side and take three slow deep breaths. Each time you inhale, focus on filling your lungs with clean, fresh air. (Pause)

As you exhale, feel all of the tension leave your lungs. (Pause)

Now stare at a spot. Look at a spot on the wall or ceiling. (Pause)

Look at that spot, breathe deep and relax. (Pause)

Your body is relaxing, deeply relaxing. (Pause)

Your eyes are getting heavy and closing down. (Pause)

You are going deep, deep, and deeper into a pleasant state of relaxation. (Pause)

Your mind is alert and aware, and your body is relaxing, perfectly. You feel good, you feel fine...you feel perfectly relaxed. (Pause)

Each and every deep breath that you take lets you relax deeper and deeper. (Pause)

Each and every sound that you hear allows you to relax deeper and deeper. (Pause)

Nothing will disturb you. Just breathe deeply and relax deeply. (Pause)

Let your body relax. (Pause)

Let all of your muscles relax as you gain control over the powerful subconscious part of our mind. (Pause)

All of your cares and troubles are just drifting away. (Pause)

You can bring them back at any time you want. (Pause)

However, it feels good to let them drift away at this time. (Pause)

But it feels good to let them drift away at this time. Each and every breath you take allows you to relax deeper and deeper each and every sound that you hear, allows you to relax deeper and deeper. (Pause)

You feel good. You feel fine. You feel perfectly and completely relaxed. (Pause)

Your mind is alert and aware and your body

is relaxing perfectly. Now allow your eyelids to feel heavy. (Pause)

Allow your eyes to feel tired. Begin to close your eyelids down tight. This will allow you to relax deeper, deeper and sounder than ever before (Pause)

You are going down deeper and sounder in this wonderful state of relaxation. (Pause)

Your mind is keenly alert and aware, and your body is relaxing perfectly. (Pause)

Now picture in your mind that with your eyes closed down tightly, you can see out of an imaginary hole in the top of your head. (Pause)

Imagine that you are looking out of that imaginary hole or window and you can see a beautiful relaxing scene around you. (Pause)

You make be picturing the night sky, or a beautiful daytime scene with mountains and trees, or a lake or the ocean shore. Or, you may be picturing a comfortable room or place that is very quiet and still. (Pause)

Whatever picture you hold in your mind, just hold it there and relax deeply and soundly. (Pause)

Now I am going to count from three down to one. With every count take a long slow deep breath. Then exhale deeply, and allow yourself to relax deeper and sounder than ever before. (Pause)

Okay, three breathing deeply, two, inhaling deeply and exhaling. Feel the tension leaving your lungs. (Pause)

One, deeper and more completely relaxed than ever before (Pause)

You feel relaxed, focused and at peace. (Pause)

Each time you practice this exercise, You

31

will find yourself relaxing to a greater and greater degree. (Pause)

Your body feels totally relaxed as your mind is keenly alert, aware and very powerful. (Pause)

You can achieve anything YOU want when you execute your own power. (Pause)

You will sleep better when its time to sleep and you will find more energy when you are awake. (Pause)

Your life is getting better and better. (Pause)

Day by day, in every way you are getting better and better. (Pause)

You feel good. You feel fine you feel totally and completely, relaxed. In a moment I am going to count from 1 to 5. (Pause)

By the time I reach 5, you will be alert and awake and feeling better than you have ever felt before. (Pause)

Each and every time you practice this exercise, you will find yourself relaxing to a greater and greater degree. (Pause)

All right, one, two, three, four, five. (Pause)

You are wide-awake, alert and feeling better in every way!

END OF EXERCISE

How do you feel? Do you feel alert and awake and feeling better than you have ever felt before?

Workshop

Activity 1 - Listen to the tape

Listen to this tape recording each day for the next 10 days. We will be adding additional self-hypnotic inductions and you will have an opportunity to listen to those as well. Our purpose is to have you condition yourself for this wonderful state of mind.

Activity 2 - Evaluate Your Induction

Record your reactions and thoughts to this exercise by answering the following questions.

What was the first thing you thought about as you finished the exercise?

How did you feel during the exercise?

How do you feel now?

Did you have any unusual sensations as you were listening to your voice?

List anything that you feel was "memorable" during the exercise.

Activity 3 (Optional) Recording the Script

Go back over the script, I prepared for you and substitute the word, *I* for the word *you*. Read into the tape recorder. Label the tape as *Chapter 3, Optional*. Listen to the newly recorded tape.

Use one of the extra *Evaluate Your Induction* forms located in Appendix A and answer the questions on the form.

Activity 4 Sharing Your Thoughts

Access the Internet and go the Self-hypnosis Forum located at:

http://www.wayneperkins.net

Share your thoughts about your first self-hypnotic experience with others from around the world. Read and learn from the responses that you see posted.

Summary

In Chapter 3, you read the FAQS, (frequently asked questions) of hypnosis and self-hypnosis. You learned more facts about the state itself. Then you actually recorded and listened to your first induction. You were the hypnotist or *operator*. You were also the subject or *hypnotee*. You completed the entire cycle of hypnosis. How do feel?

Chapter 4 Your Hypnotic Experience

"I can't look in his eyes," stated the Associated Students President as she introduced me before my Concert of Stage Hypnotism at a small Illinois college.

This was my first college audience with many psychology students and even a psychology professor in attendance. I was thinking how strange it is to mention hypnosis with these learned men and women. These learned men and women are fearful and think I have some strange powers over people, with the use of my eyes. Why do people have this prejudice about hypnotism and eyes?

Eyes have always been a significant part of the hypnosis process. What is the connection the eyes and hypnosis? The sense of "sight" acts as a metaphor for hypnosis.

At the count of three, look up from this book. Scan your eyes around the room, keeping a finger on your place in this book. Then focus your attention on one object on the other side of your room. Focus on this object for about ten seconds and then start reading the book again. All right, one, two, and three, look, scan and focus.

Well, that was fun. Did you notice as you scan around your room all the different objects? Did you notice different textures, sizes, shapes, form, mass, and colors? As you focused on one object did you notice what happened? Other objects, shapes, sizes, form, mass, and colors go out of focus. They recede into the background. They don't seem quite as distinct or as important anymore. This experience, the experience of sight is just like hypnosis.

With hypnosis you focus your attention so much on a central word, thought or idea that the rest of the world goes out of focus. You don't really notice or care that much about what else is going on around you. You know that people are talking or that things are happening but they aren't as important as the ideas your are concentrating on at the time. With hypnosis you don't need your eyes open at the beginning of the induction in order for it to *work*. Later in this chapter you will learn how to hypnotize yourself with an Eyes-Closed Induction. It will be fun!

Objectives of Chapter 4

The objectives of Chapter 4 are to help you understand what to say to yourself during the hypnotic induction. You will learn Perkins 7-Steps To A Successful Induction. You will also learn why you should say certain words and phrases. You will learn what words and phrases to use during an induction. There will be more explanation in Chapter 14, Hypnotism Theory, when you are interested. You will learn to record and execute the Eyes Closed Method of Induction.

What Do You Say During The Induction?

What is an induction? What do you say during the induction? An induction is the formal ceremony with a goal to elicit a hypnotic response from the subject or hypnotee. The subject or hypnotee may carry out the formal ceremony normally presented by a hypnotist. Hypnosis can and does exist even without the formal ceremony or induction. This concept is hard for people to understand. But it is true. Once you accept this teaching self-hypnosis will become powerful and it will be fun to use.

The induction is a signal that *hypnosis is coming*. You had better get ready! This is when your belief system and your expectation come into clear focus.

What do you say during the induction? I will list the basic parts of a typical induction or ceremony, for you. This will include what you do and what you say to yourself. The following is Perkins 7-Steps To A Successful Induction.

Find a quiet spot to relax: This also includes time of day as well as a physical site. Find a time and a place such as a comfortable chair or bed to sit or lie down.

Pre-hypnotize: Tell yourself what you want to accomplish during this session. Say to yourself what you need to accomplish 3 or 4 times.

Induction: The induction you used in Chapter 3 was the Eyes-Open Method. You are now going to use the Eyes-Closed Method of Induction. You begin with eyes closed.

Deep breathing suggestions: Tell yourself to breathe deeply to enhance the relaxation response.

Imagination stimulation: Wrap your imagination around a specific idea or healing thought. This is also called the hypnotic prescription or prevailing thought.

Post-hypnotic suggestion: Give your-self a suggestion during the induction that will predict and ask for a particular behavior, once you awaken from hypnosis.

Awakening: Give yourself a signal to come out of self-hypnosis. It may be a count, such as from one to five. It may also be a set amount of time. For example, you may tell yourself that you will concentrate in hypnosis for 2 minutes and then awaken on your own, feeling wide-awake and alert.

Why Do You Say it?

Question: Why do we find a quiet spot?
Answer: We find a quiet spot to eliminate as many distractions as possible. Hypnosis is a state of focussing on one thought and eliminating many others. You may also hypnotize yourself walking though a crowded mall with hundreds of people talking and making noise.
Question: Why do we use pre-hypnosis?
Answer: We use pre-hypnosis to remind ourselves of the precise behavior we want to change. If we fall into natural sleep during the induction, we will still accomplish our goal. Our pre-hypnosis will

	act as the hypnotic prescription or prevailing thought.
Question:	Why do we use an induction?
Answer:	We use an induction to get our mind ready for change. The induction is a formal ceremony devised to send a signal that we are ready for change.
Question:	Why do I use deep breathing exercises?
Answer:	You can use deep breathing to give yourself methods of relaxing you generally don't think about in the waking state. You also give yourself a method of getting feedback to your brain that the suggestions are taking effect.
Question:	Why do I want to stimulate my imagination?
Answer:	You stimulate your imagination because everything is possible in your imagination. Think about when you dream at night. You can fly, slay dragons or run faster than any human being. You can interact with people who have died several years before and you can be any age. Everything is possible in your imagination. Why not focus on all the possibilities?
Question:	Why do I use a post-hypnotic suggestion?
Answer:	You use a post-hypnotic suggestion as your main theme or reason for the session. You carry out these suggestions after the hypnotic session is over. If your goal is to control your weight, then your post-hypnotic suggestion would involve words and ideas that will help you control weight. You may tell yourself to begin exercising or drinking water. If your goal of the session is to relax then your post-hypnotic suggestion will involve how you will feel relaxed after the induction session. You may suggest feeling the same degree of relaxation while you are working on a project.
Question:	Why do I need to awaken myself if I am not

really asleep?

Answer: By giving yourself a cue to awaken, you are giving yourself a signal that it is okay to resume your everyday activities. It also acts as a symbol to remind yourself that something unique and wonderful was happening to you for a few minutes in your day. The hypnotic induction is a ceremony to remind you to cue yourself for change. The awakening ceremony is a ceremony to cue yourself to return to the state of mind that existed before the ceremony.

Are you ready for more fun!

Let's go!

Self-hypnosis Induction 2: Eyes Closed Method

Find a great place to sit or lie down and relax. Again, you will be talking into your voice-recording device. You will listen and then evaluate. Remember to add three seconds each time you see the word "pause" as you are recording.

Remember to use the word "you" when recording this information to yourself. You may then work with using the word "I" and substitute it for "you" later on.

BEGINNING OF INDUCTION

Get comfortable sitting in your chair or lying down on your bed or couch. As you sit in your chair or lie on the bed or couch, you are going deep, deep, and deeper into relaxation. (Pause)

You will accomplish deep relaxation today. (Pause)

Close your eyelids down tight, shutting out the light. (Pause)

As you close your eyelids down, shutting

out the light, your body is relaxing deeply. (Pause)

In a moment, you are going to take three slow, deep breaths. (Pause)

Each time you inhale, draw the air in slowly and deeply. (Pause)

Each time you exhale, focus on pushing all the tension out of your lungs. (Pause)

As you breathe in the fresh, clean air, you feel relaxed and satisfied. (Pause)

One, inhale slowly, take a very deep breath. Hold it for a moment. (Pause)

Now exhale, (Pause) let all the tension leave your body. (Pause)

Two, inhale slowly, and as you exhale, feel the tension leaving your lungs. (Pause)

Three, inhale slowly, and as you exhale, feel all the tension leaving your body, and all of the tension, leaving your lungs. (Pause)

As you exhale, you feel all of the tension leaving your lungs and all of the tension leaving your body. (Pause).

Nothing will disturb you, just focus on your deep, peaceful, relaxation. (Pause)

Your mind is alive and alert, and your body is relaxing deeply, soundly and perfectly as if you were in a deep, sound, sleep. (Pause)

All of your muscles are letting go as you go deeper into this pleasant relaxation. (Pause)

Your mind is keenly alert and aware, as your body is relaxing perfectly. (Pause)

Each and every muscle and fiber in your body is relaxed, as you go deeper and deeper into the self-hypnotic state of mind.

Your mind is always keen and alert, and your body is relaxing deeply and soundly. (Pause)

Now that that your body is completely relaxed, your mind is focused on the suggestions I give you. (Pause)

Picture in your mind that you are looking at the night sky. (Pause)

Picture the night sky complete with stars and planets and a full moon, or you may picture the sky with no stars and planets and no moon at all. (Pause)

Whatever sky you picture in your mind will be the correct one. (Pause)

Now right in the middle of the night sky, picture a large wheel. (Pause)

It can be a wagon wheel or automobile wheel or bicycle wheel. (Pause)

Whatever wheel you picture in your mind will be the correct one.

Now as you picture the wheel in your mind, imagine that the wheel is turning. (Pause)

Let it turning clockwise or counter clockwise, fast or slow. Just imagine it turning. (Pause)

As the wheel is spinning and turning, you are going deeper and deeper into the hypnotic state of mind. (Pause)

Your mind is keen and alert, as your body is relaxing perfectly. (Pause)

Each and every deep breath is allowing you to relax deeply. (Pause)

Each and every sound that you hear is allowing you to relax very deeply. (Pause)

Now begin to drop the thoughts of the night sky and the wheel. You will now prepare to emerge from this wonderful state of mind. (Pause)

In a moment I am going to count from one to five. At the count of five, you will be wide-awake and alert and feeling better than you have ever felt before. (Pause)

If you are listening to this tape just before you are going to sleep at night, you will be able to turn off the tape and go to sleep immediately. (Pause)

Waking up when you want to, feeling alive and alert and better than you have ever felt before. (Pause)

If you need to be awake after listening to this tape, you will be wide-awake and alert and feeling better than you have ever felt before. You will have energy that will last all day. (Pause)

When you go to bed later, you will be able to sleep all night and feel very rested in the morning. (Pause)

All right, one, beginning to emerge from hypnosis, two feeling better than you have ever felt before, three, four, get ready now, five, wide awake, alert, feeling great in every way. Yawn, stretch, feel good!

END OF INDUCTION

How do you feel? Wasn't that fun? I hope you enjoyed it.

Workshop

Activity 1 - Practice Your Induction

Listen to this tape recording each day for the next 10 days. Alternate with the induction you listened to in Chapter 3. We will be adding additional self-hypnotic inductions and you will have an opportunity to listen to those as well. Our purpose is to have you condition yourself for this wonderful state of mind.

Activity 2 - Evaluate Your Induction

Record your reactions and thoughts to this exercise by answering the following questions.

1. What was the first thing you thought about as you finished the exercise?

2. How did you feel during the exercise?

3. How do you feel now?

4. Did you have any unusual sensations as you were listening to your voice?

5. List anything that you feel was "memorable" during the exercise.

Activity 3 - Recording the Script (Optional)

Go back over the script, I prepared for you and substitute the word, "I" for the word "you." Record into the tape recorder. Label the tape, Chapter 4, Optional. Listen to the newly recorded tape.

Use one of the extra "Evaluate Your Induction" forms located in Appendix A, and answer the questions on the form.

Activity 4 - Sharing Your Thoughts

Access the Internet and go the Self-hypnosis Forum located at: http://www.wayneperkins.net

Share your thought about your second self-hypnotic experience with others from around the world. Read and learn from the responses that you see posted.

Activity 5 - List Perkins 7 Steps to a Successful Induction
1.
2.
3.
4.

5.
6.
7.

Summary

This was a lot longer exercise, in order to condition you for a more profound experience. You entered the self-hypnosis experience using the Eyes Closed Method. You learned the Perkins 7-Step Method to a Successful Induction. You also learned what to say and why you say it, during a hypnotic induction.

I hope you enjoyed Chapter 4. You are beginning to enjoy the art of self-hypnosis. It is very beneficial for you.

Chapter 5 How To Write A Hypnotic Prescription

Lisa was frustrated. For years she had been an excellent sales representative but now has problems increasing sales and her personal income. As a sales representative who was successful in the past, she could find no technique that would help her now. Even though she was making more sales presentations than ever before, the sales and income just weren't happening. The harder she tried, the more frustrated she became.

Finally, Lisa decided to create a *hypnotic prescription* or *prevailing thought* and use it before every sales call. She told herself that every time she greeted a customer or prospect, she would imagine that person exactly like her in every way. She imagined that person looking for love, recognition and respect. Instead of focusing on a tangible product, Lisa would focus on the customer's personality. Instead of visualizing the customer as just another sale, the customer would be seen as a living, loving person, just like Lisa. The customer wanted to be respected and appreciated. The customer wanted Lisa to valued his opinion.

After only two weeks after creating and exercising this new hypnotic prescription or prevailing thought, Lisa began to achieve great results. Lisa was also making new, lifelong friends. Work was fun. Now, that Lisa was making sales and making friends, her appreciation of her job and her life was heightened.

Objectives of Chapter 5

What is a hypnotic prescription? What are the magic words you say to yourself to achieve results? How can you integrate the prescription into your personal success plan?

There are three objectives to Chapter 5.

You will understand what is a hypnotic suggestion or prevailing thought.

You will learn how to create your own hypnotic prescription or prevailing thought.

You will apply your own prescription to your self-hypnosis induction.

Let's begin!

What Is A Hypnotic Prescription?

Question: What is a Hypnotic Prescription or Prevailing Thought?

Answer: A hypnotic prescription or prevailing thought is the script or verbiage that you use during the hypnotic ceremony or induction that centers on one or more of your goals. This prescription may include a story or metaphor that helps explain a lesson that the subconscious mind understands and acts upon. The prescription is written in such a way that your subconscious mind will act upon it either during the hypnotic state or after the induction when the hypnotic experience is officially over (The posthypnotic state). The prescription can be very lengthy or administered in one well-chosen word. The prescription works best when repeated many times. The hypnotic prescription or prevailing though when administered goes into your powerful subconscious mind. It changes your belief system from one of *I can't* to one that states, "I can."

Always Administer Positive Words and Ideas

Question: Would you rather listen to something positive or

47

something negative?

Answer: Our brains are crammed full of negative ideas and scripts. How many movies have you seen with death, destruction, and loss of love and heartache? How many newscasts have you observed examples of mans' inhumanity towards man? How many times did we run those scripts in our minds when parents, relatives, or friends told us we would never amount to anything, or we should be grateful for what little we have? These hypnotic Prescriptions (yes, they are hypnotic prescriptions) keep running in our head and may be affecting our behavior and our attitudes toward successful and healthy lives. People think themselves to life and they think themselves to death. How many people do you know with negative attitudes that also have poor health? Have you ever met a person with a negative attitude that is not achieving what they want to achieve in life? Do they put down and ridicule people that are successful? Do they act resentful to everyone and everything? You are going to learn how to be positive so you can overcome all of those negative attitudes and scripts. Since we already have enough negative scripts running in our brains, we need to load a pile of positive ones to our memory. We are so use to reacting to things negatively that I am going to show you specific examples of *goals* stated by my clients that needed to be changed from negative to positive before goals were achieved.

The following is a list of goals stated by my clients in a negative way and the corresponding words or statements that they changed in order to accomplish their goals. My self-hypnosis students created these positive prescriptions on

48

About the Author

Wayne F. Perkins, is a Certified Clinical Hypnotherapist and Stage Hypnotist who resides in Phoenix, Arizona.

Wayne presents his *How to Hypnotize Yourself Without Losing Your Mind*, public workshops and to business groups and associations throughout the country.

Along with teaching Self-hypnosis Wayne presents workshops on Hypnotic Past Life Regression and Stress Management. He has personally developed techniques in Pain Management, and has worked with people suffering from life threatening illnesses. Wayne has developed exercises to stimulate the immune system.

In addition Wayne F. Perkins has presented his Concert of Stage Hypnotism, to high schools and colleges for over 20 years. In his demonstrations he uses all volunteers from the audience. Wayne entertains and helps students overcome test anxiety.

Wayne also gives sales training to companies and teaches sales professionals how to hypnotize their clients as well as how to apply powerful goal achievement skills and self-hypnosis with professional selling. Wayne has over 16 years as a successful sales professional and sales trainer.

Wayne F. Perkins, is Certified by the American Board of Hypnotherapy and received his training at the American Institute of Hypnotherapy, and the Hypnotism Institute of Chicago.

Wayne taught Business Education at Elgin High School in Elgin, Illinois from 1972-1975. He received his Bachelor of Science in Business Education from Northern Illinois University in DeKalb, Illinois. He taught Self-hypnosis for Self-improvement at Triton College in River Grove, Illinois.

You state a behavior you want to change or goal you wish to achieve during the session or after the session.

You state it in a way that assumes you have already reached the goal or are rapidly getting closer to achieving it.

In the case of controlling your weight, you may say something like this:

> "Each day I find my-self looking better and better. I enjoy the way I am controlling my weight and the way I look."

Then, you may talk to yourself in a way that assumes you are already in possession of the goal. For example:

> "I am achieving my ideal weight. My friends and relatives are in complete support of the way I look now. I feel healthier and happier than I have ever felt. I am relaxed and self-confident. My confidence builds daily. I celebrate in my success!"

For each of the above examples of prescriptions think of examples of hypnotic scripts or prescriptions. How do these examples relate to the challenges that you are facing? Do you feel that you would be too unrealistic with yourself to visualize and tell yourself that you are already in possession of these goals? Why do you feel that way?

If you feel that way you are normal. It takes some time to finally convince ourselves that we are everything we should be rather than everything we think we are not. Reality is in the eyes of the beholder. I have witnessed people achieving extraordinary accomplishments when logic and reason would dictate that they couldn't possibly achieve these goals.

When I taught Business Education classes at Elgin High School, in Elgin, Illinois, I remember having a student in class with many personal problems at home. By all circumstances this student should have become a drop out and perhaps a burden on

society later on.

Due to a positive self-esteem, however, she was able to achieve straight "A's" in high school. She was a National Merit Scholar, worked part time, lived in a very abusive home, and had to raise her younger brothers and sisters. She accomplished all of this and with an IQ of 80. Fortunately, no one told her the test score.

You have the power to raise your self-esteem regardless of the conditions you face in life. The power of your belief will be enhanced and illuminated through the hypnosis induction, conditioning exercises and your custom prescription or script. You are the main ingredient, however, in making it all work!

How Do You Integrate A Prescription in an Induction?

This is the easy part! Remember when I said that ALL hypnosis is self-hypnosis? If you don't remember from the book so far visit my FAQ link located on the Internet at:

http://www.wayneperkins.net

Since ALL hypnosis is self-hypnosis, then WHEREVER you decide to place your custom prescription or script, this is going to be the correct place. How can you lose? Just to give you a head start, however, I am going to give a few tips on where it may fit in quite nicely.

As you are giving yourself instructions, such as, "As you sit up in your chair or lie down on your bed, you are seeing yourself in your perfect weight."

Another place a script may fit in nicely is after you say, " breathe deeply, and relax and push all the tension out of your lungs." You may insert something like, "I am calm and relaxed while taking tests." (This is from the test anxiety example in the preceding table)

A great spot to insert your custom script is just before you

emerge from the state. For example: "When I emerge from this state of mind, I will feel better than ever before."

A plan to incorporate hypnotic prescriptions or scripts in your life is much like planning a speech or a paper for school. In a speech or paper, you are supposed to tell them what you want to tell them, tell them, and then tell them what you told them. This is what is called the power of threes. Concentrate on telling them what you want to tell them. Then, tell them. Finally tell them what you told them, as you complete Activity 1, Create Your Hypnotic Prescription.

Workshop

Activity 1 - Create Your Hypnotic Prescription

Create a hypnotic prescription or prevailing thought based on your most pressing need or desire in life. State it in positive terms.

Activity 2 - Record Your New Induction

I am going to repeat the first induction we performed together in Chapter 3. Before you read it into your recorder, I want you to edit it by writing down prescription statements relating directly to your problem or goal. Then insert those statements anywhere you feel necessary in the induction text. Feel free to mark up your textbook as you insert your positive statements in your induction. You may even use different colored ink or a highlighter to make it easier to work with as you record the induction.

Note: From my experience and background, telling yourself the behavior you want, followed by strong, positive statements reinforcing that behavior, is your quickest guarantee for success.

Self-hypnosis Induction: Eyes Open Method.

Always remember that ALL hypnosis is self-hypnosis! You are always in control. You have all the power necessary to make positive changes in your own life. You may have found out already in life that you also have the power to make all the negative changes in your life. Let's focus on the positive changes.

Find an area in your home or place of work where you can

have about 10 minutes to yourself. That's right, only 10 minutes are needed in your quest for a successful induction at this point. After practicing this exercise many times, you may reduce the time to only one or two minutes. Now read the following words into a recording device. Read very, very slowly. Pretend that you are tired as you read this exercise and you will react in a relaxed, sleepy, manner. (You may want to print out this page for future reference) Whenever you see the (Pause) cue, pause for 3 seconds, then go ahead and read again. Let your body relax for a few moments before continuing on.

BEGIN INDUCTION

Sit up in a comfortable chair or lie on a couch or a bed with your hands resting in your lap or by your side and take three slow deep breaths. Each time you inhale, focus on filling your lungs with clean, fresh air. (Pause)

As you exhale, feel all of the tension leave your lungs. (Pause)

Now stare at a spot. Look at a spot on the wall or ceiling. (Pause)

Look at that spot, breathe deep and relax. (Pause)

Your body is relaxing, deeply relaxing. (Pause)

You eyes are getting heavy and closing down. (Pause)

You are going deep, deep, and deeper into a pleasant state of relaxation. (Pause)

Your mind is alert and aware, and your body is relaxing, perfectly. You feel good, you feel fine...you feel perfectly relaxed. (Pause)

Each and every deep breath that you take lets you relax deeper and deeper. (Pause)

Each and every sound that you hear allows you to relax deeper and deeper. (Pause)

Nothing will disturb you. Just breathe deeply and relax deeply. (Pause)

Let your body relax. (Pause)

Let all of your muscles relax as you gain control over the powerful subconscious part of our mind. (Pause)

All of your cares and troubles are just drifting away. (Pause)

You can bring them back at any time you want. (Pause)

However, it feels good to let them drift away at this time. (Pause)

But it feels good to let them drift away at this time. Each and every breath you take allows you to relax deeper and deeper each and every sound that you hear, allows you to relax deeper and deeper. You feel good. You feel fine. You feel perfectly and completely relaxed. (Pause)

Your mind is alert and aware and your body is relaxing perfectly. Now allow your eyelids to feel heavy. (Pause)

Allow your eyes to feel tired. Begin to close your eyelids down tight. This will allow you to relax deeper, deeper and sounder than ever before. (Pause)

You are going down deeper and sounder in this wonderful state of relaxation. (Pause)

Your mind is keenly alert and aware, and your body is relaxing perfectly. (Pause)

Now picture in your mind that with your eyes closed down tightly, you can see out of an imaginary hole in the top of your head. (Pause)

Imagine that you are looking out of that imaginary hole or window and you can see a beautiful relaxing scene around you. (Pause)

You make be picturing the night sky, or a

beautiful daytime scene with mountains and trees, or a lake or the ocean shore. Or, you may be picturing a comfortable room or place that is very quiet and still. (Pause)

Whatever picture you hold in your mind, just hold it there and relax deeply and soundly. (Pause)

Now I am going to count from three down to one. With every count take a long slow deep breath. Then exhale deeply, and allow yourself to relax deeper and sounder than ever before. (Pause)

Okay, three breathing deeply, two, inhaling deeply and exhaling. Feel the tension leaving your lungs. (Pause)

One, deeper and more completely relaxed than ever before (Pause)

You feel relaxed, focused and at peace. (Pause)

Each time you practice this exercise, You will find yourself relaxing to a greater and greater degree. (Pause)

Your body feels totally relaxed as your mind is keenly alert, aware and very powerful. (Pause)

You can achieve anything YOU want when you execute your own power. (Pause)

You will sleep better when its time to sleep and you will find more energy when you are awake. (Pause)

Your life is getting better and better. (Pause)

Day by day, in every way you are getting better and better. (Pause)

You feel good. You feel fine you feel totally and completely, relaxed. In a moment I am going to count from 1 to 5. (Pause)

By the time I reach 5, you will be alert and

awake and feeling better than you have ever felt before. (Pause)

Each and every time you practice this exercise, you will find yourself relaxing to a greater and greater degree. (Pause)

All right, one, two, three, four, five (Pause)

You are wide-awake, alert and feeling better in every way!

END OF INDUCTION

How do you feel? You are rapidly gaining control over the problem you listed above and many more problems you may not have thought of yet!

Activity 3 - Evaluate Your Induction

Record your reactions and thoughts to this exercise by answering the following questions.

What was the first thing you thought about as you finished the exercise?

How did you feel during the exercise?

How do you feel now?

Did you have any unusual sensations as you were listening to your voice?

List anything that you feel was "memorable" during the exercise.

Activity 4 - (Optional) Recording the Script

Go back over the script, you prepared and substitute the word, "I" for the word "you." Record into the tape recorder. Label the tape, Chapter 5, Optional. Listen to the newly recorded tape.
Use one of the extra *Evaluate Your Induction* forms located in the appendix, and answer the questions.
Activity 5 - Sharing Your Thoughts
Access the Internet and go the Self-hypnosis Forum located at:

http://www.wayneperkins.net

Share your thoughts about your third self-hypnotic experience with others from around the world. Read and learn from the responses that you see posted.

Summary

58

In Chapter you learned how to create a hypnotic prescription or prevailing thought. Every time you wish to begin a new project in helping yourself achieve a new goal, use the format presented in this chapter.

You learned how to integrate your prescription or prevailing thought, in your induction and you listened to it for your success programming. We will continue on in Chapter 6 in positively communicating your goals to your subconscious mind.

You are doing just fine.

Chapter 6 How to Put More Power in Your Prescription
Jane

Jane had listened to hypnosis tapes and meditation tapes to help overcome stress. However, the only time she was in a stress-free environment was when she was at home away from the situations that "trigger" the stress. Work was stressful. Abusive bosses and co-workers created stress. Jane did not have enough time to finish any assignment successfully. This caused stress.

As an alternative to her hypnosis treatment, Jane decided to use more visualizing in her hypnosis prescriptions. As she hypnotized herself she began to picture the ideal job and surroundings. She pictured bosses and co-workers with happy faces and cheerful attitudes. The images became so clear in her mind that her own attitude changed as she went off to her regular job every day. Jane projected that she would be in charge of her mind and her life.

William James, a great philosopher who was quoted near the end of the last century, said," The greatest discovery in my lifetime is that man can change his life, by changing his mind."

Soon, a job came up in a different department in another building. Jane decided to apply for the position. Jane was hired and noticed on the very first day that her new job would be drastically different. There wasn't as much stress in the assignments. Her bosses were kind, considerate, and supportive. Her co-workers were wonderful people with only positive things to say about other people. There was very little gossip. Jane's new job was almost exactly as she visualized it during those many weeks that she hypnotized herself with her new, *graphic* prescription.

Will your personal prescriptions and prevailing thoughts work better by adding graphics? Will your life improve by simply *changing your mind*? Let's find out!

Objectives of Chapter 6

The objectives of Chapter 6 are for you to learn *hypnotic graphics*. What are hypnotic graphics and how can they help you? Also, you will be creating hypnotic graphics for your next self-hypnosis induction. This will fun and very enjoyable! Let's begin!

The Hidden Meanings of Your Subconscious Mind

There are many hidden meanings in located in your subconscious mind. By *hidden*, I mean that our subconscious mind reacts differently to words than we realize in our consciousness. Sometimes those hidden meanings will have a negative effect on us instead of the positive effect we are looking for. It's strange that we don't receive an owner's manual for our brain. It certainly would help.

Sometimes a friend will tell you a joke that is really a put down. For example, "Boy, do you look ugly." The friend may not have an intention of creating displeasure for you. However, the subconscious mind will accept the comment as fact. Over time, statements like "boy do you look ugly!" may hurt your self-confidence in other social situations.

You may begin to feel poorly about yourself in an area that was of no concern before. Even it you know for a fact in your conscious mind that you are beautiful, the ugly statement drives itself home. It affects behavior regarding your looks and may affect other behaviors as well. For example you may begin to dress poorly and forget to take care of your physical features. You may consciously act out on what your subconscious has accepted.

Parents, as well meaning as they may be, often make statements in anger or frustration aimed at their children that only serve as weapons that cripple the child once adulthood is reached. Spiritually and physically, the child will be hurt. Some parents may tell a child that they may never amount to anything. They may tell their child that they are not as smart or athletic as their other brother or sister.

Parents take note of this: Always say positive, uplifting statements in front of your children. What you say in front of your children is going to be what your children say in front of their children and what their children say in front of their children. The chain goes on and on, forever. The cycle can only be broken through your efforts.

Another area of concern of which to be aware is the phenomena associated with *organ language*.

Organ language refers to the way our body and subconscious mind responds to certain words and phrases. Just as eating too much of the same food daily may cause an allergy, saying a word or phrase to ourselves may cause our bodies to respond in unusual ways.

Here is a true story of a case I worked on, over twenty years ago. Bob had severe lower back pain. He went to a medical doctor and chiropractor, but could achieve only, temporary relief. No matter what medication was prescribed, Bob had a difficult time sitting at his desk and also moving about the office.

Finally I decided to see if I could help. I asked him to tell me what was bothering him. Bob would talk about the stress he was receiving on the job and how his boss was a "pain in the ass." Every time Bob talked about his boss he kept saying he worked for a "pain in the ass." Bob also said his job was a "pain in the ass."

I talked to Bob about organ language and suggested that when he talked about his boss or job, that he choose another colorful phrase that didn't refer to body parts or possible diseases.

Bob thought that advice made sense and gave it a try. It was

Printed in the United Kingdom
by Lightning Source UK Ltd.
9569500001B

their own, during one of my self-hypnosis workshops.

Goal Stated Negatively	Hypnotic Prescription or Prevailing Thought, Stated Positively
I want to lose weight	I am in control of my weight
I have to stop eating	I eat only healthy foods
I want to quit smoking	I am a non-smoker
I don't want to stay awake all night	I will sleep soundly, all night long
I need to stop freezing up while taking tests	I am calm and relaxed while taking tests
I want to stop hitting my little brother	I am nice to my little brother

It is truly amazing how you will change your habits and change your life by changing just a few words in your speech and your thought patterns. The above list can go on forever.

Think of a few goals right now. Make a "T" on a piece of paper or in this textbook. On the left side write down your prescription in negative terms, on the right, state your goal in a positive way.

Can you see or feel a difference? You will, in a very short time!

What Do You Say In A Prescription?

What are the magic words that will help you achieve all of your goals? Where do I find the right things to say? How do I say them? Let's find out.

In a prescription you say two basic things.

49

hard, however, for Bob to find an appropriate substitute in his daily language. Instead, Bob stopped talking about his boss in a negative way. He stopped talking about his boss, altogether. Twenty years have gone by now, and Bob and his boss are best of friends. By the way, Bob's lower back pain ended the day of our discussion about organ language.

There was no formal hypnotic induction or ceremony given. There was no posthypnotic suggestions given. Bob subconscious mind took control in a waking state.

Have you ever said, "This job gives me a headache" or "This person makes me sick."? Have you ever heard of anyone referring to a broken heart? Listen to yourself and others. Learn and master the language of your body and your subconscious mind. The mind you save, may be your own.

Adding Graphics to Your Prescription or Prevailing Thought

Do you remember the phrase, "A picture is worth a thousand words?" It applies to all aspects of hypnosis including the most important part. Without a great hypnotic prescription or prevailing thought, hypnosis is just another relaxation technique.

Pictures or hypnotic graphics in this case, involve more than just your visual field. When I talk about pictures and graphics in the hypnosis context, I am talking about sight, sound, touch, taste, smell, intuition and emotional feelings.

Did you ever watch a stage hypnotist in action? If you did, you may have noticed how the hypnotist altered all the senses listed above. To the degree you can integrate "pictures or graphics" in a self-hypnosis session, you will achieve results at an accelerated pace. The images you create with your imagination will turn into reality. The images you create will also guarantee a pleasurable hypnosis session.

The following are examples of graphics you can use to spice up your hypnotic prescription:

Goal	Graphic Embedded in Your Prevailing Thought or Prescription
Weight control	I see myself at work at my ideal weight. My boss and several co-workers are smiling at me and congratulating me on my success.
Self-confidence	Mary tells me I am an inspiration to her. I feel great. I am calm and confident as I give my speech. I practically run to the stage when I am introduced because what I have to say is so important. I see the audience applaud when I make my important points and I hear them congratulate me after my performance. I am calm and confident as I think about my speech.
Healthy immune system	I feel great. My body is working while I am at rest to repair all of the damaged cells in my body. I see in my mind a control room filled with dials and switches. I walk over to the switch that is labeled "respiration" and I set it for "deep breathing." All of my cells are being energized. I feel healthy.

Improved memory	In my mind I hear the songs of my youth. A particular song and a scene in my mind of what I was doing while listening to that song is very clear. All of the people I was involved with at that time are clear in my mind's eye.
Sound sleep	Sleeping is fun for me. Each night when I hit the pillow, my body begins to relax, instantly and completely. The feeling of the sheets and blankets next to my body act as triggers to send me into a deep, quiet state of relaxation. As I breathe deeply and relax, all of the peaceful air around me enters my body. As I exhale, all of the tension leaves my body and goes out into space. Traveling out into the darkness of deep space. All of the sounds of the night lull me to sleep like the effects of a lullaby.
Stress reduction or relaxation management	I can smell the soothing smell of pine trees as I deeply relax. Nearby I hear the sound of a stream as the water washes over the rocks. I see the peaceful blue sky with fluffy white clouds and feel a soft warm breeze across my shoulders. I feel very relaxed.

One way to improve your graphic representations during hypnosis is to cut out pictures in magazines and newspapers that are most representative of the way you want to look and feel. Paintings on a wall or a particular song that you want to listen to, help as well. Fragrances of flowers or scented candles may assist your prescriptions by stirring up other positive visual images buried in your subconscious mind.

Collect pictures, drawings, and remember sounds, smells, and tastes that are pleasing to you. Then, incorporate them into your self-hypnosis prescriptions or prevailing thoughts.

Workshop

Activity 1 - Let's Create A Powerful Prescription!

Think about your problem or goal: the problem or goal that you are working on for this class. What pictures or graphics do you feel will help you and encourage you to achieve success? Write them down in the following spaces. I will leave you space for a few, but feel free to make copies of this page or your use your additional copy in the appendix of this book.

Activity 2 - Adding Graphics To Your Hypnotic Prescription or Prevailing Thought

In the space below, paste or tape a picture taken from a magazine, newspaper, photograph or computer print out. This is a graphic that best depicts your goal or goals. Make several copies of this page or use the form located in the appendix. Someday you may have more goals and challenges that you will conquer using these techniques.

Activity 3 - Integrating Graphics In Your Self-hypnosis Plan

I am going to give you the Eyes Closed Induction Method. This is the very same induction that you recorded earlier. Before you begin to record, read the induction to yourself and pick spots where you will insert the graphics. I will leave some blank lines on the sheet for your editing. You may insert your graphics there or in any spot you feel necessary. Remember that you are always the best hypnotist for your problems. When you need help refer back to the table located in this chapter.

Read the following induction and insert your graphics. Record your edited version. As you read the graphics into the recorder, try and visualize your personal graphics. Listen to your new induction for a period of two weeks. You may also listen to any other induction method you enjoy as well.

The Eyes-Closed Method of Induction With Added Hypnotic Graphics

BEGINNING OF INDUCTION

Get comfortable sitting in your chair or lying down on your bed or couch. As you sit in your chair or lie on the bed or couch, you are going deep, deep, deeper into relaxation. (Pause)

Close your eyelids down tight, shutting out the light. (Pause)

As you close your eyelids down, shutting out the light, your body is relaxing deeply. (Pause)

In a moment, you are going to take three slow, deep breaths. (Pause)

Each time you inhale, draw the air in slowly and deeply. (Pause)

Each time you exhale, focus on pushing all the tension out of your lungs. (Pause)

As you breathe in the fresh, clean air, you feel relaxed and satisfied. (Pause)

One, inhale slowly, take a very deep breath. Hold it for a moment. (Pause)

Now exhale (Pause)

Let all the tension leave your body. (Pause)

Two, inhale slowly, and as you exhale, feel the tension leaving your lungs. (Pause)

Three, inhale slowly, and as you exhale, feel all the tension leaving your body, and all of the tension, leaving your lungs. (Pause)

As you exhale, you feel all of the tension leaving your lungs and all of the tension leaving your body. (Pause).

Nothing will disturb you, just focus on your deep, peaceful, relaxation. (Pause)

Your mind is alive and alert and your body is relaxing deeply, soundly and perfectly as if you were in a deep, sound, sleep. (Pause)

All of your muscles are letting go as you go deeper into this pleasant relaxation. (Pause)

Your mind is keenly alert and aware, as your body is relaxing perfectly. (Pause)

Each and every muscle and fiber in your body is relaxed, as you go deeper and deeper into the self-hypnotic state of mind. Your mind is always keen and alert, and your body is relaxing deeply and soundly. (Pause)

Now that that your body is completely relaxed, your mind is focused on the suggestions I give you. (Pause)

Picture in your mind that you are looking at the night sky. (Pause)

Picture the night sky complete with stars and planets and a full moon, or you may picture the sky with no stars and planets and no moon at all. (Pause)

Whatever sky you picture in your mind will be the correct one. (Pause)

Now right in the middle of the night sky, picture a large wheel. (Pause)

It can be a wagon wheel or automobile wheel or bicycle wheel. (Pause)

Whatever wheel you picture in your mind will be the correct one. Now as you picture the wheel in your mind, imagine that the wheel is turning. (Pause)

Let it turning clockwise or counter clockwise, fast or slow. Just imagine it turning. (Pause)

As the wheel is spinning and turning, you are going deeper and deeper into the hypnotic state of mind. (Pause)

Your mind is keen and alert, as your body is relaxing perfectly. (Pause)

Each and every deep breath is allowing you to relax deeply. (Pause)

Each and every sound that you hear is allowing you to relax very deeply. (Pause)

Now begin to drop the thoughts of the night sky and the wheel. Drop the thoughts of the hypnotic graphics. You will now prepare to emerge from this wonderful state of mind. (Pause)

In a moment I am going to count from one to five. At the count of five, you will be wide-awake and alert and feeling better than you have ever felt before. (Pause)

If you are listening to this tape just before you are going to sleep at night, you will be able to turn off the tape and go to sleep immediately. (Pause)

Waking up when you want to, feeling alive and alert and better than you have ever felt before. (Pause)

If you need to be awake after listening to this tape, you will be wide-awake and alert and feeling better than you have ever felt before. You will have energy that will last all day. (Pause)

When you go to bed later, you will be able to sleep all night and feel very rested in the morning. (Pause)

All right, one, beginning to emerge from hypnosis, two feeling better than you have ever felt before, three, four, get ready now, five, wide awake, alert, feeling great in every way. Yawn, stretch, feel good!

END OF INDUCTION

How do you feel? Let's evaluate your session.

Activity 4 - Evaluate Your Induction

Record your reactions and thoughts to this exercise by answering the following questions.

1. What was the first thing you thought about as you finished the exercise?

2. How did you feel during the exercise?

3. How do you feel now?

4. Did you have any unusual sensations as you were listening to your voice?

5. List anything that you feel was "memorable" during the exercise.

Activity 5 Optional: The Self-hypnosis Forum

Go on-line to the Self-hypnosis Forum located at:

http://www.wayneperkins.net

Compare notes with other students from around the country and around the world.

Summary

In Chapter 6, you learned how graphics can be an integral part of your self-hypnosis plan. Refer to this chapter when you need to create powerful hypnosis scripts in the future.

Chapter 7 A Profound Self-hypnosis Experience

How is your progress so far? Have you defined your goal? Are you listening to your prescription each night? Are you still excited about the process of self-hypnosis?

By now, you have had success in self-hypnosis assignments. Your subconscious is ready to take on more and help you solve your problems and achieve all the success you wish for in life.

This chapter is going to be a fantastic one for you!

Objectives of Chapter 7

Chapter 7 will introduce a more profound self-hypnosis experience. You may have already experienced profound self-hypnosis but I will introduce some additional tools maximize your experience. You have two main objectives to this chapter.

1. Experience a more meaningful and interesting self-hypnosis experience.
2. Pretend you are a Hypnotherapist and create self-hypnosis prescriptions for three cases. This will give you a chance to exercise your new mental muscle.

Now get ready to learn more on how you can enhance your self-hypnosis experience!

More Meaning with Music

Remember my definition for hypnosis? Hypnosis is the extraordinary power words have when surrounded by our complete attention.

Is music an important part of your life? Do you enjoy

listening to music while you work, study or relax? You may want to include music to enhance your hypnotic experience. Are you aware how music fits into that definition? When you are happy do you ever listen to your favorite music? When you are sad do you ever desire to listen to a sad song? When people have major breakups in relationships, many times they request sad songs.

I was a nightclub musician for three years and found that statement to be true. Many times a man or a woman would tell me their sad story and cap it off by requesting a very sad song! I didn't understand why until I became a hypnotist. I believe that by asking for the sad song the person is extending the ceremony of the altered state of mind that she/he is in. Why not enhance or extend the ceremony of your hypnotic induction the same way. Your mind and body are craving to act as one. Music will help provide the harmony you need in creating and enhancing this experience.

Say It with Flowers

Since you are aware that music may help you enjoy your self-hypnosis experience, you may ask, "What about the sense of smell? Can fragrance help enhance our experience?"

Yes, it can. Many times when a person visualizes a scene in the mountains or in a garden, he/she will tell me that they could actually smell the flowers. In a visualization I use with people suffering from live threatening diseases, I ask my clients to picture an old kitchen with home made bread baking in the oven. Many times, the client will say afterwards that they can actually smell the bread. That smell may linger, even after the induction is over.

Again, the subconscious mind and the imagination are working to enhance the experience. If you can voluntarily add something to effect the sense of hearing or the sense of smell, you may enjoy a more profound hypnotic experience.

At Thanksgiving, Christmas, or other special feasts, does

your home take on a unique smell? Special foods that are only eaten during holidays have smells associated with them. How do you personally feel when you enter a home at this special time of year. Does it help your enjoyment of the holiday or does it bring back bad memories of times when expectations were never met?

When you enter movie theatre and smell popcorn or a sporting event and smell the food that is offered there, do you react to it emotionally? Do the smells of special events help enhance the experience for you?

If you answer "yes" to any of the above questions, you may find that by inserting new smells into your hypnosis experience, you will enhance the overall experience significantly.

Where do you find these smells? Pleasant smells can be found from a variety of resources. Various soaps and room fresheners help bring in new smells and new experiences. You may want to burn candles, incense, or scented oils that you find pleasing or relaxing. As your sense of smell is reacting positively to these smells, your body will be relaxing deeper than ever before. The effects of the relaxation may continue long after the hypnosis session is over, just as the smell of the room will linger for sometime after you leave it.

A Touching Experience

When I hypnotize someone in a workshop or in a stage setting, I always like to use the sense of touch to deepen and enhance the experience. This is done when I address the subjects sitting on stage, concentrating in hypnosis. I say, "In a moment I will touch you on your back, and as I do, you will go deeper into hypnosis." Many people are *kinesthetic*. They *feel* their world as opposed to *seeing* it. Have you ever listened to people engaged in conversation? When one person is replying to a statement in agreement, he or she may add, "I know what you are talking about, or I have a feel for it." This person is telling you that they experience their life using their sense of touch as a primary tool.

If the person responds to the statement in agreement with, "I see what you mean, or I get the picture," he/she may be telling you they see their world through their sense of sight.

In everyday communications, we go back and forth in viewing our world through our senses. As we concentrate on an idea or concept, we tend to choose using one sense as a primary assistant in concentrating. If you find your are a visual person, then incorporate a great deal of meaningful visuals in your inductions. If you are a tactile or kinesthetic person, incorporate a lot of feelings in your work. Use music to enhance your auditory world and fragrances to bring your sense of smell to your aid in concentrating and focussing.

Use as many of your senses as you can in working to produce self-hypnosis. You will greatly enhance your goal achievement experience.

Powerful Eyes Open Induction Method

We will record a powerful eyes open induction method. This method is designed to help you feel like you have been hypnotized. Too, many times, people give up in their quest to master self-hypnosis, because they want a more dreamy like state or more profound experience. The truth is that even with the lightest stage of self-hypnosis, you can achieve the greatest results. Repetition is the chief ingredient of success. The more you practice reaching your goals, the better you get. The self-hypnosis program gets easier and easier.

As I present this new induction method, my prescription will focus on having you learn the process faster, easier and in a more powerful way. After reading, recording, and listening to your induction method, you will create prescriptions for each of the three case studies included later in this chapter. You will play the role of the clinical hypnotherapist. Are you ready? Let's begin.

You will read your script into your tape recorder and to listen to it, in a few minutes. You may want to find some relaxing music or sounds of nature. Use a scented candle, incense, or another smell of your choosing that will represent a relaxing smell. Find a very comfortable chair or bed, where you · can actually feel the fabric or sense the texture and softness of the chair or bed as it braces against your muscles. Feel the air if you have a fan as it brushes against your skin. Use your senses to enhance your hypnosis experience.

We will invoke a new and more profound self-hypnotic experience. Your eyes will be open, but instead of gazing at a spot on the wall or ceiling, you will be watching the flickering flame of a candle.

BEGINNING OF INDUCTION

Now, sit up in your chair and set the candle at a point that when you watch the flickering flame, your eyes are elevated slightly. (Pause)

As you watch the flickering flame of the candle, you are feeling very relaxed. Take 3 slow, deep breathes. (Pause)

As you inhale, feel your lungs expanding. (Pause)

As you exhale, feel all of the tension, leaving your lungs. (Pause)

Now breathe deep and relax. As you relax stare at the candle and watch the flickering flame. (Pause)

As you watch the flame, your eyes may feel a burning sensation and want to close. (Pause)

As you feel the sensation or if your eyes feel tired, close down your eyelids tightly, relaxing deeply. (Pause)

Now, with your eyes closed down tightly, notice how you still see the image of the flame of the candle. (Pause)

Relax deeply now. Deeper than ever before. (Pause)

Concentrate on relaxing all the muscles of

your forehead. As you relax the muscles of your forehead, you find your self, relaxing deeper and sounder than ever before. (Pause)

Drop the image of the flickering flame of the candle and instead picture a soft white light, emanating from high up above your head and shining down on top of your head. (Pause)

As this white light shines upon your head, allow all your facial muscles to relax. (Pause)

This is a deeper relaxation than ever before. (Pause)

Now allow the soft white light to glow upon your back and your chest. (Pause)

As the soft white light glows upon your back and your chest, your body relaxes deeper and sounder than ever before. (Pause)

Allow the light to cover your arms, stomach, chest and your legs, relaxing each muscle as it travels down your body. (Pause)

You feel good, you feel fine. You feel perfectly and completely relaxed. (Pause)

Each and every breath that you take is relaxing every muscle in your body. (Pause)

Each and every sound that you hear is relaxing every muscle in your body. (Pause)

You feel good, you feel fine, and you feel perfectly and completely relaxed. (Pause)

Now picture yourself walking in a larger forest. It is a beautiful forest with lots of beautiful trees, bushes and flowers. (Pause)

As you walk through the beautiful forest, you are going deeper and sounder in this pleasant state of relaxation. Mind alert, and body relaxing, perfectly. (Pause)

As you walk through the beautiful, you notice a field of beautiful flowers up ahead. (Pause) As you see the beautiful flowers, you notice how wonderful they smell. (Pause) These are flowers that are pleasing to your body. (Pause)

As you walk closer to the beautiful smelling flowers you pick a few flowers. (Pause)

You begin to feel the petals in your fingers and in your hands. (Pause)

As you place the flowers in your hand, your body is relaxing deeper, and sounder than ever before. (Pause)

Now as you gaze at the petals of the flowers in your hand, you may notice that you can hear the distant sound of a running stream or river. (Pause)

The sound of the running water assists you in relaxing very deeply. (Pause)

More deeply and soundly relaxed than ever before. (Pause)

As you walk through the forest you realize that you learn very quickly. (Pause)

You learn concepts and principles very quickly after your self-hypnosis exercises. (Pause)

Now remember the flower you placed in your hand. (Pause)

Think about its color, shape and size. (Pause)

As you think about the flower, allow it to become a symbol of your increased learning and understanding abilities. (Pause)

When you emerge from self-hypnosis, remember the flower and its power to help you learn and understand. (Pause) Think about it often when you need to learn something difficult in the future. (Pause)

Now I am going to count from one to five. (Pause)

With every count, you will be more and more aware. When I reach five, you will be wide awake, alert, feeling energetic and better than you have ever felt before. (Pause)

Each and every time you listen to the self-hypnosis induction you will go deeper and gain more benefits from the experience. (Pause)

Okay. One, get yourself ready to emerge from this relaxing state. Two, all feeling returning to your body. Three, your breathing is returning to the aware state. Four get ready to emerge now. Five, wide awake, feeling good, yawn and stretch.

END OF INDUCTION

How do you feel? Thank you for your concentration. I hope you had an amazing journey. Practice this induction often and you will achieve many amazing results.

Workshop

Activity 1 - Evaluate Your Induction

Record your reactions and thoughts to this exercise by answering the following questions.

1. What was the first thing you thought about as you finished the exercise?

2. How did you feel during the exercise?

3. How do you feel now?

4. Did you have any unusual sensations as you were listening to your voice?

5. List anything that you feel was *memorable* during the exercise.

81

Activity 2 - You Are The Hypnotherapist

You are well on the road to achieving all of your goals in life! How exciting! How would you like to help others achieve success as well?

The following three case studies represent three real cases of mine that were helped with the power of self-hypnosis. I want you to read the case studies, then develop a self-hypnosis induction and prescription for each. As you teach you shall learn. You will find this a very rewarding experience.

After you have read the cases studies and created the scripts, take out a fresh cassette and record your script as if this script was meant for you. Then, listen to your script. If you need more evaluation forms, make copies of the one above or the ones located in the appendix of this book.

Good luck and enjoy the exercise!

Case Study 1. Lack of Self-confidence

Here is a case I would like you to work on. Pretend you are the hypnotist and instructor of self-hypnosis. Pick one of the induction methods you have worked with. Then create a hypnotic prescription for that induction that will help our friend, Bob. (Bob is not his real name but this case is a real one taken from my files).

Bob, is 45 years old. He has worked in the electronics field as a technician for the last 15 years. He is coming to you because of your reputation of solving your problems and achieving your goals with self-hypnosis. Bob has just been laid off his job and feels he has nothing to offer the world as far as skills to take another job. Bob is creative and intelligent, however, he is having a hard time getting past the fact that he has had the same job for many years and is afraid to put together a resume and actively seek employment.

Case Study 2. Afraid Of Flunking

Dr. Susan Jones, (this is a made up name but was a real case) is a Surgeon with about 10 years experience working in the medical field. Dr. Jones needs to become certified to practice at a group of hospitals in Salt Lake City. Even though Dr. Jones has been a top student throughout her educational career, she is very apprehensive about taking the written and especially the oral examination. Dr. Jones will be taking the test in a nearby hotel conference center.

She has heard of all your accomplishments using self-hypnosis, and is wondering if you could help her learn self-hypnosis for overcoming test anxiety. If she does not become board certified in Salt Lake, she could face financial ruin in a very short time.

Case Study 3. Procrastination

Pavel wants to begin writing a book. Pavel is very intelligent and very capable of writing a book. However, you uncover that when Pavel was a small child, his father told him he would never grow up and do anything important. Pavel's father's exact words were, "Pavel, you will never amount to anything."

For this exercise, I want you to recommend a hypnotic induction that you feel would be correct for Pavel and create a hypnotic prescription.

Activity 3 - Self-hypnosis Forum

Go to the self-hypnosis forum located at: http://www.wayneperkins.net and compare notes with other students from around the world. How did you enjoy the role of the Hypnotherapist?

Summary

Chapter 7 challenged you to add more elements to your hypnotic experience. By introducing more sensory activities you were able to experience a more profound hypnotic condition. Each time you listen to your induction with the added elements you will achieve a more profound experience. Keep practicing!

Chapter 8 How To Achieve All of Your Goals

Is self-hypnosis always enough to help you achieve all of your goals? What happens if you stop setting aside time each day for your programmed relaxation and goal setting using hypnosis? Is it time to toss this book?

Beverly

Beverly was feeling ill. She had a very abusive boss. Every night she would complain of headaches. Although she achieved many goals through self-hypnosis, she could not find enough motivation to use it on her situation at work. She tried not to think of work when she came home. However, the harder she tried not to think of her abusive boss, the harder it was to relax and get rid of the thought. Beverly needed something else to help her get over the problem.

Beverly decided that the best way to handle the problem was to "forgive" her boss. Maybe by forgiving her boss and dismissing his actions she could go home at night and focus on more important aspects of her life.

Within a week, her headaches were gone. She wasn't thinking about work when she was at home and then started working on more meaningful personal goals.

Within six months, Beverly received a promotion and moved over to another department where everyone treated her well.

Sometimes self-hypnosis may just not be enough.

Soon we will discuss how we "bury the dead" when it comes to abusive relationships or abusive situations. Like Beverly, when you bury the dead, you will bring life to all of your personal goals.

While you were completing the activities in Chapter 7, did you wonder why I gave it to you? Did you wonder why I asked you to step in the role of the hypnotherapist and perform his/her function?

Have you ever suffered from a lack of self-confidence?

Were you ever afraid of something when logic and experience tell you there is no reason to be afraid?

Did you ever procrastinate?

Since ALL hypnosis is self-hypnosis, do you know why I gave you the assignment?

There is no hypnotist, or therapist better trained to help you achieve your goals, than the therapist called your subconscious on unconscious mind.

We are training your subconscious mind to rehearse a positive outcome for some very common challenges you are facing or will face.

Your answers are always the correct answers.

Objectives of Chapter 8

During this chapter you will learn about the obstacles that are being placed before you in your self-hypnosis journey. You will learn how to overcome them. You will also begin on my 5-Step Goal Achievement Program. This plan may be used with or without a self-hypnosis induction. Let me state that one more time.

This plan may be used with or without a self-hypnosis induction.

"My mission in life is to help you achieve your mission in life." Use the next three chapters to achieve your mission in life.

Obstacles To Self-hypnosis Success

Many times you may start a self-improvement plan only to find it to collapse in a few hours, few days, or a few weeks. Why does this happen? Are we somehow too weak to make a plan work for us?

The two major causes of a self-improvement plan not working for us lies in two applications for the same word. That one word is expectation." Since success in improving ourselves involves taking us away from our "comfort zone," thoughts of failure creep from our conscious mind down to our subconscious or unconscious mind. We wrap our attention around those failure thoughts and soon our prescription for success is defeated. We go back to our old, however familiar thoughts and ideas.

Another cause of a self-improvement plan not working is from the "expectation" others have about our new behavior. Strangely enough, our family members and friends express these thoughts and ideas. The people that really love us, express either verbally or non-verbally that we will fail.

Since one of the reasons we want to improve is because of the benefits they will receive, its strange that they will not support us with the faith and belief that we need during this time.

I personally believe that since we are moving out of our friends' expectation of behavior for us, it puts all of our friends into an uncomfortable position. It takes some of their power away.

If you believe as I do that this condition may be fatal to your success in life, you will be able to take the appropriate steps.

Plough The Road: Obstacle Removal

How do we remove the obstacles in our path of success? Here is a method I found that seems to work well. Remember that as we change, others will change. We need to initiate the change.

At the end of this chapter, focus on Activity 1., Who Stands In Your Way. Think of one of your greatest challenges or your most meaningful goal.

Write down the names of people that may give you a

negative reaction as you discuss your goal with them. For example, a negative reaction may be "Oh, I tried losing weight by hypnosis, but I put more weight on than ever before." Another one may be, why is it important for you to get good grades in school." "Look at all I have accomplished in life and I was a school drop out."

Once you have written down these names in the far-left column, look at the middle column. List the negative statements as you receive them. Expect the negative statements. They will come. If you can't quote the person directly, perhaps they have a typical response. List that typical response.

In the third column, make up an imaginary statement that will modify the negative statement in column two.

For example, for the first negative statement of, "Oh, I tried losing weight by hypnosis, but I put more weight on than ever before," add the following statements in the right column: "I believe in you and your success." "I could have made the hypnotists plan work, however, I just wasn't ready at the time." Your success will give me new hope."

Plough the road of the many obstacles in your path and success will be as easy as achieving the self-hypnotic state.

Introduction to Perkins' 5-Step Achievement Program

Have you started another New Year only to revert back to all of your old habit patterns and limitations? Do you ever wonder if you will ever become the person you know you deserve to become? Do you really want to achieve all of you goals in life?

This is the first of a five part series called "Perkins' 5-Step Goal Achievement Program."

It is designed to augment your self-hypnosis exercises in order to guarantee the success of your hypnotic prescriptions.

This program will assist you in achieving all of your goals. The five parts of my plan on helping you achieve all of your goals are:

1. Bury the dead
2. Write it down
3. Create an image book or treasure map
4. Create and participate in a success support group
5. Become a mentor

Each part of my plan can be a stand-alone prescription for success. Using any combination of parts will vastly improve your success. We will learn the first step in this chapter and continue with the other steps in succeeding chapters.

Step 1 - Bury The Dead

Have you ever been hurt physically, emotionally or spiritually by anyone? Do you still harbor ill feelings toward those that hurt you? Do you feel unworthy of the potential success that seems out of your grip?

You need to "bury the dead."

In Beverly's story, early in this chapter, she decided to bury the dead by not paying attention to her boss.

Burying the dead is burying all negative feelings you are directing toward another person, another group or another experience. When we harbor and nurture bad feelings towards others we actually turn those negative dreams or desires towards ourselves.

William James, at the turn of the 20th Century stated that "whatever we hold in our mind, our body begins to move toward."

According to the principles of hypnosis practice we understand how this affects us as we center our thoughts on a goal. However, do we really fully comprehend how thoughts or ideas fixated towards others can lead to the same result?

For example, many scientists believe that thoughts are energy. As we direct these thoughts or energy towards personal goals, we start physically, emotionally, and spiritually, moving towards the desired result.

When we send these same thoughts or energy towards others, do we help others also reach their goals?

I believe we do.

If you believe in this theory, than is it not possible to send negative thoughts or energy towards those who have harmed us? If we do send these negative thoughts or energy towards others, aren't we also setting ourselves up for the same result?

Maybe, this is why many religions and philosophies around the world, state that we should love our enemies and only wish on another person what we would wish for ourselves.

Let us begin to practice that right now.

Practice by spending a few minutes each day, going over in your mind experiences with a person who has harmed you in some way. As you visualize this person, feel deep forgiveness for that person. Breathe deeply and relax a few moments as you reminisce. Wish for that person the same love and success that you yourself wish to receive in life. Forgive that person and forgive yourself for feeling in a negative way towards him/her.

Abraham Lincoln once stated, "the quickest way to defeat an enemy is to make that enemy your friend." In your mind, let's make that enemy your friend. You both have so much to gain by the experience.

You will achieve all of your goals in life.

Activity 1 - Who Stands In Your Way

List the names of people you may feel stand in your way, blocking your path to your goals. Place those names in the first column. In the second column list any statements they made to you which shows how little they believe in you. In the third column change or modify the negative statement in column 2 to reveal how you would really want to hear it.

Begin after the example given.

A Healing Exercise

(This is an example of a goal stated as: I want to go into business for myself)

Name Of The Person Who Stands In Your Way	What The Person Said To You As You Explained Your Goals	What You Really Want That Person To Tell Your Regarding Your Goal Achievement
Julio	I tried that business and failed. Its impossible to succeed in the business you wish to enter.	I believe you are on the right track. I tried that business once but wasn't as enthusiastic as you. Let me give you some of my contacts. They will love you.

Read and record the healing induction below. Remember to use all of your senses. You may wish to use music, uses a fan, or notice the softness of your bed or chair before you drift off into this wonderful state of mind.

Use everything you have to heal the hurt projected by others. We will make this induction short and sweet, so you can reinforce it many times during the day.

Get comfortable. Make sure your tape is recording. Let's begin.

BEGINNING OF INDUCTION

With your body relaxed focus your attention and your eyes on a fixed object. Take a deep breath, drinking in life sustaining oxygen and breathe out immune inhibitors. (Pause)

Feel at one with your body. Your body is relaxing, deeply relaxing. (Pause)

All of your muscles are going loose, limp and deeply relaxed. (Pause)

Nothing will disturb you, just listen to the sound of my voice. (Pause)

Each and every time I suggest sleep or relaxation to you, (Pause)

You will go deeper and sounder into this deep, healing state of mind. (Pause)

Your mind is alert and aware, as your body is relaxing deeply. (Pause)

Your eyes are beginning to feel tired. I am going to count from five down to one. You may close your eyes at any time but by the time I reach one, close your eyes down tightly, this will assist you in relaxing very, very deeply. (Pause)

Your mind is alert and aware but your body

92

is relaxing, perfectly. (Pause)

Five, four, three, eyes getting heavy, closing down, two, closing down, one, close your eyes down tight, shutting out the light. (Pause)

You are relaxing more with each and every breath that you take and every sound that you hear. (Pause)

Each and every deep breath is sending you deeper and sounder into this pleasant state of mind, your healing state of mind. (Pause)

You are here in the Present Moment, relaxing and feeling good. (Pause)

Your mind is alert and aware and your body relaxing, deeply. You feel good, you feel fine, and you are perfectly, relaxed. (Pause)

Concentrate on relaxing the muscles of your forehead. (Pause)

Picture in your mind that you can actually see the muscles of your forehead and as you think about these muscles. (Pause)

You feel them relax. (Pause)

You may even feel a tingling sensation come over your forehead. (Pause)

Let that sensation travel down to your face, your neck, your chest, and your stomach. (Pause)

Relaxation is traveling down to the long muscles of your legs. (Pause)

It's going all the way down to your feet. (Pause)

Now think about your feet for a moment. Picture in your mind that you an actually see the muscles in your left or right foot. (Pause)

Watch as the muscles in your left or right foot relax. (Pause)

.Let go. Go limp at the thought. (Pause)

Your legs and feet are totally relaxed.

(Pause)

They are responding to your total concentration. (Pause)

Each and every deep breath that you take is sending you deeper and sounder into hypnosis and healing. (Pause)

Each and every sound that you hear is sending you deeper and sounder into this beneficial state of mind. (Pause)

Nothing will disturb you, just listen to the sound of my voice. (Pause)

Each and every time I suggest relaxation to you now or in the future, your relaxation will become deeper and more pronounced. (Pause)

You feel calm and confident and filled with the self-satisfaction for becoming master of your mind and master of your body. (Pause)

As you relax, picture in your mind that you are looking at the night sky. (Pause)

You can imagine it complete with stars and planets and with a full moon or crescent moon, or with no moon or no stars at all. (Pause)

Whatever sky you imagine is the correct sky. (Pause)

Now, somewhere in that night sky I want you to imagine a large wheel. It can be a spoke wagon wheel or a bicycle wheel or an automobile wheel. (Pause)

Any wheel you picture is the correct wheel. (Pause)

As you picture this wheel, your body is relaxing, deeply relaxing. (Pause)

All of your muscles are going loose and limp and relaxed. (Pause)

Now as you see the wheel projected in the night sky, make the wheel start turning. (Pause)

It can go slow or fast but in any case, have

94

the wheel move. (Pause)

You may also want the wheel to move toward or away from you.

As it moves toward you it gets bigger and bigger. As it moves away from you, it seems to get smaller in the night sky. (Pause)

As the wheel moves your body relaxes deeply. (Pause)

Now, as you are imagining the wheel in the sky turning and moving, hold the images in your mind and begin counting backward to yourself from 100 down to 1. (Pause)

Count at this speed. One hundred, ninety-nine, ninety-eight, ninety-seven, and so on. (Pause)

Keep counting and as you do you will go deeper and deeper into hypnosis. (Pause)

Your subconscious mind is listening to each and every suggestion I give you and you will find your life is changing in a very positive and beneficial way. (Pause)

Keep counting. (Pause)

Relax. Go deeper and sounder into this pleasant state of relaxation. (Pause)

Even though we have been relaxing for just a few minutes, when we are finished it may seem that you have slept deeply for a very long time. (Pause)

You will have a very long and beneficial sleep for your body. (Pause)

Keep counting backward slowly, picturing the wheel in the sky. (Pause)

As you do, you are relaxing perfectly, feeling good. (Pause)

When you emerge from this session, you will feel better then you have ever felt in your entire life. (Pause)

Breathe deep and relax. (Pause)

Take in the life sustaining oxygen, and exhale, pushing out all hatred, jealousy, distress, anxiety, and all negative emotions. (Pause)

You can always get them back easily enough, but the are not required for proper healing. (Pause)

Replace these negative emotions with hope, love, forgiveness, and confidence. (Pause)

With every breath that you take, feel the healing grow. (Pause)

You have complete control over this process. (Pause)

Now stop counting and be still and know. (Pause)

Relax and see the images before you. (Pause)

The wheel, the night sky, and any other images that you require are still in your mind. (Pause)

Relax now and let go of those images. (Pause)

Clear your mind. (Pause)

Just breathe deep and relax. (Pause)

In a moment we will emerge from this wonderful healing state of mind. (Pause)

In the future each and every time you want to go into this healing state of mind you will be able to do so by just closing your eyes and turning your thoughts within. (Pause)

Turn your thoughts within by thinking about your breathing, focusing on an object, or by just closing your eyes and thinking about the night sky. (Pause)

You are always in control of your healing thoughts. (Pause)

I am going to count from one to five.

(Pause)

With every count you become more aware of everything going on around you. (Pause)

By the time I reach five, you will feel alert, awake, energetic and aware. You will feel great in every way. (Pause)

When you go to sleep tonight, you will sleep soundly and perfectly. (Pause)

What may have been bothering you before this session tonight will cease to bother you as you sleep. (Pause)

You will awaken tomorrow feeling alive, alert and energetic. (Pause)

One you are beginning to emerge from this state. Two, slowly easily, and gently you are feeling better than ever before. Three, you are becoming more aware and alert. Four, eyes beginning to open, and five, eyes open. You may want to yawn or swallow. (Pause)

You are feeling energetic and refreshed.

END INDUCTION

How do you feel?

Activity 3 - Evaluate Your Healing Induction

Record your reactions and thoughts to this exercise by answering the following questions.
1. What was the first thing you thought about as you finished the exercise?

2. How did you feel during the exercise?

3. How do you feel now?

4. Did you have any unusual sensations as you were listening to your voice?

5. List anything that you feel was "memorable" during the exercise.

Activity 4 - Healing Induction 2, Eyes Closed Method

BEGIN INDUCTION

>Close your eyes down tight, become still and relaxed. (Pause)
>
>With your eyes closed, breathe deep and relax. (Pause)
>
>With your eyes closed down tightly, pretend that you can look up and see out of a window located on your forehead. (Pause)
>
>Roll your eyelids up under your eyelids and hold them there as you allow your body to relax.

(Pause)

We are going to take three slow, deep breaths. (Pause)

As you inhale, let all the life sustaining oxygen into your lungs. As you exhale, push out all tension and stress. (Pause)

Let go of anything that is blocking your immune system. (Pause)

All right, one, breathe in, hold it. Breathe out, pushing out all the tension in your lungs. (Pause)

Two breathe in. hold it. Now push out all the tension in your lungs. (Pause)

Three, breathe in, hold it, and now let go of all your tension. (Pause)

Your body is relaxing, deeply relaxing. (Pause)

Let your body relax, floating down into the security of your chair. (Pause)

Let your mind stay alert and aware. (Pause)

As you are relaxing, focus your attention on any sounds that you are hearing in the background. (Pause)

As you do, you find these noises pleasing and relaxing as well. (Pause)

Wouldn't it be interesting to be able to increase the volume of the external sounds by just thinking about them? (Pause)

As you do make the sounds louder you find your body sinking down into the security of you chair. (Pause)

You are sinking down, drifting down. (Pause)

You may feel a light or heavy sensation and this sensation begins to assist you in relaxing deeply. (Pause)

Feel more deeply relaxed than ever before.

(Pause)

Nothing will disturb you, just listen and concentrate on the sound of my voice. (Pause)

Now wouldn't it be interesting to decrease or diminish the peripheral sounds around us? As we decrease these sounds, we find ourselves going deeper and sounder in this pleasant state of relaxation. (Pause)

Your mind is alert while your body is relaxing perfectly. (Pause)

You feel good, you feel fine, and you feel perfectly relaxed. (Pause)

Now concentrate on the sound of my voice. (Pause)

As you do, you find yourself going deeper and sounder into hypnosis. (Pause)

Your mind is alert and aware but your body is relaxing perfectly. (Pause)

Healing is beginning, now. (Pause)

Imagine, picture in your mind that you are looking at a big, red barn. (Pause)

This barn is located on a farm, much like you may have seen in the East or Midwest. (Pause)

Picture yourself outside the barn on a farm, looking out at the barn. (Pause)

The sky in this setting is big and blue with big puffy, white clouds. (Pause)

As you picture the barn in your mind, your body relaxes deeply. (Pause)

You feel, good, you feel fine, you feel perfectly, relaxed. (Pause)

Each and every breath that you take is sending you deeper and sounder into this pleasant state of mind. (Pause)

Near the barn, picture a farmhouse. It can be a white or gray farmhouse, a new or old farmhouse. (Pause)

Whatever farmhouse you picture in your mind is the correct one. (Pause)

As you picture the farmhouse in your mind, you body relaxes perfectly. (Pause)

You feel good, you feel fine, and you feel perfectly, relaxed. (Pause)

Now, picture yourself walking toward the farmhouse and as you near the screen door, you begin to smell the pleasant aroma of homemade bread. (Pause)

This smell is coming from the kitchen area of the farmhouse. (Pause)

Inside the kitchen you notice the table and chairs, the sink and the stove. (Pause)

Now picture next to the stove, a lovely, elderly woman who is smiling at you. (Pause)

This person may resemble someone you know or don't know, but picture the woman smiling at you. (Pause)

This is a woman who is totally at peace and harmony with everyone she meets. (Pause)

You may have met a person like this before. (Pause)

This woman is totally loving and forgiving. (Pause)

She loves you and every one around her, unconditionally. (Pause)

The homemade bread and food she is preparing is for you and you alone. She wants you to become healthy and strong. (Pause)

She is sincere with her love and understanding of your problems.

You feel safe and secure around her. (Pause)

Before eating she is going to take you back outside the house and show you the farm. (Pause)

As you walk out of the house, she takes your hand and shows you the different fields on the farm. (Pause)

There are fields of corn as far as the eye can see. (Pause)

There are other fields and cow pastures in other directions that are abundant in plant life. (Pause)

This is a place where life abounds. (Pause)

You feel good, you feel fine, and you feel perfectly, relaxed. (Pause)

Each and every cleansing breath that you take is sending you deeper and sounder into this pleasant, healing state. (Pause)

Now for a few moments I want you to continue on your journey into this quiet, safe, healing place. (Pause)

Picture everything on the farm as vividly as you can. (Pause)

Then I will begin, again (PAUSE FOR A FEW MOMENTS)

You feel good, you feel fine, you feel perfectly, relaxed. (Pause)

Nothing will disturb you, just listen to my voice. (Pause)

Now begin to let the images of the woman and the farm to fade from you mind. (Pause)

You feel good about the experience. (Pause)

In a moment I am going to count from one to five. (Pause)

When I reach five, you will feel wide-awake, alert and aware.

Tonight, when you go to bed, you will sleep soundly and deeply. (Pause)

The images of the farm, the woman, life and healing will enter your sleep. (Pause)

This will enable you to sleep better than you

102

may remember. (Pause)

Each and every time you use this exercise, you will become more and more at east with it. (Pause)

You are becoming master of your mind and master of your body.

All right, one, slowly easily and gently you are beginning to become more aware, two... gently moving toward becoming awake, three we are almost there, four, get ready, and five, wide awake and alert.

Feeling good in every way.

Have a fantastic day!

END INDUCTION

Activity 5 - Evaluate Your Induction

Record your reactions and thoughts to this exercise by answering the following questions.
1. What was the first thing you thought about as you finished the exercise?

2. How did you feel during the exercise?

3. How do you feel now?

4. Did you have any unusual sensations as you were listening to your voice?

5. List anything that you feel was "memorable" during the exercise.

Summary

During this chapter you learned the two major obstacles in success of your self-hypnosis self-improvement plan. You also learned an excellent method of defeating those obstacles. The introduction of Perkins' 5-Step Goal Achievement Program and the first part, "Bury the Dead," was discussed. You also received two great methods of using self-hypnosis to heal your mind and spirit. Practice those often and you will feel wonderful.

Chapter 9 Advanced Goal Achievement Techniques
John

In Jack Canfield's and Mark Victor Hansen's original *Chicken Soup for the Soul*, I am reminded of the short story called "Another Check Mark On the List." This is a story about a 15 year old boy named John who, on one rainy day, when it was too wet outside to play, he decided to write a list of goals. John continued writing until he had 127 goals. These goals included exploring the Nile River, climbing high mountain peaks around the world and learning 3 foreign languages. He also wanted to be featured in a Rose Bowl Parade and play several musical instruments.

Of the 127 goals that he listed over 60 years ago, John has achieved 108. If he lives to become 75 years old he will achieve 109 (he listed "live to see the 21st Century"). How did John achieve all of these goals? He wrote them down.

Objectives of Chapter 9

Sometime during your self-hypnosis training and working to achieving your goals, you may not feel motivated. As a matter of fact, several times during your goal achieving exercises you may feel this way. You may be finding yourself reverting back to your same bad habits.

"My mission in life is to help you achieve your mission in life."

By now you have achieved some success using the self-hypnosis principles I gave you. Now its time to give you my 5-Step Goal Achievement Program. With the 5-Step Program you will incorporate techniques that employ little use of a formal self-hypnosis induction but will achieve fantastic results for you just the same. You may work the plan independent of your self-hypnosis exercises or combine the two. You will achieve amazing and quick, positive results.

Step 2 Write It Down

Write it down, write it down, write it down!

Have you ever got to a point where you were going to write down a New Year's Resolution or some other goal you thought you wanted, only to find yourself procrastinate. One year later, were you faced by the same New Year's Resolution or goal? Why does this happen? It happens because of that little voice inside of you that says, "I am not good enough or worthy enough to be in possession of the benefits derived from achieving my goal." You have been programmed for failure.

I recently read a motivational quote that said: "If you can't write it down, you can't do it." Let's think about that for a minute. Every day you may be compiling lists of things to do to run your household, perform your job, or plan your business trip or vacation. How many times do you really write down, exactly what you want out of life? How many long term or short-term goals do you write down?

When you hypnotize yourself, you want to focus your attention on specific words and ideas and give those words and ideas your complete attention.

Did you ever write a letter, business report or term paper and at times find your fingers flying across the keyboard or across the notepad or stationary? Since written words are symbols of objects, ideas or feelings, could the physical process of entering these words onto a page actually create the hypnotic condition? I believe it does. When you use language to communicate on paper, you need to process the information on a subconscious level. It's too hard to think of every single word, phrase, idea, and then try to put all of those ideas into a logical format, one letter or sound at a time. The help you are getting while creating is coming straight from your powerful subconscious mind. Why not take advantage of another chance to use your powerful subconscious mind, by writing down your goal?

Write it down in your day planner, write it down and hang it on your walls, write it down on sticky notes and place them on your bathroom mirror or on your windows. Every time you write your goal down, your body is moving toward your goal. The goal is getting clearer and clearer. The roadmap you create by writing it down is projected straight to your subconscious mind and is being acted upon.

Picture this

A popular syndicated cartoonist would writes down 15 times a day, every day that "I want to be a syndicated cartoonist." He does this every single day, even when he doesn't exactly feel like a syndicated cartoonist. Now, Scott Adams, the creator of the "Dilbert Cartoon" is a full-time, syndicated cartoonist, known the world over. Scott wrote it down.

One way to state that goal in a more positive and immediate context is to say, "I AM a syndicated cartoonist." Act as if you already are in possession of the goal. It takes a lot of pressure off you during your daily activities and also conditions you to feeling the role and getting comfortable with it.

One day I found myself studying to become a hypnotist. I would write down each day, "I am a professional hypnotist." Now, I am a hypnotist. My subconscious mind was okay with me being a hypnotist long before my conscious mind was ready to accept the idea. It will happen like that for you too. What helped me expedite my career was by writing it down.

Write your goals down everywhere. The very fact that you are reading and listing this information is a great start toward overcoming the real obstacles and moving forward toward achieving all of your goals. Think about John, the 15-year-old goal achiever from *Chicken Soup for the Soul*. Now that he is 74 years old, what advice would John have for you when you ask

him: "What was the most important thing you can do to achieve your goals?" John would say, just three words.
Write it down.

Stephanie

Stephanie was looked upon to as a picture of motivation. She used self-hypnosis techniques in her quest to have the perfect weight. She only ate healthy foods and exercised 5 to 6 days a week. Then one day, she skipped her self-hypnosis session. She decided that the weather wasn't good enough to go jogging. Stephanie decided that she would eat fast food burgers with extra French fries. The next day and the next, she continued to skip her self-hypnosis, stop exercising and eat junk food. Stephanie was now feeling poorly and gaining weight. What could she do to get back on track?

Stephanie then began to cut out pictures of women in health and fitness magazines. She cut out figures of women who were approximately her height and weight. She then took a scissors and cut off the heads of these pictures and then pasted them on construction paper and hung them on her bedroom wall. Within three days, Stephanie was back to exercising. She was eating healthy foods and practicing her self-hypnosis for relaxation. Stephanie was back on track!

Step 3 Create An Image Book Or Treasure Map

What would I say if you challenged me by asking, "If you have 10 minutes to come up with the most powerful technique of achieving a goal, what would that one technique be?" If I had only had one opportunity to persuade someone that they will be helped in life, this is the technique I would teach. I would teach them to create an image book or treasure map.

Have you ever heard how a picture is worth a thousand words? You will definitely shortcut your time in becoming successful by creating an image book or treasure map.

What is an image book or treasure map?

An image book is a page or series of pages or sheets of colored paper that you place pictures of items you wish to acquire. It may also include text of motivational statements or headlines that spell out the goals you wish for yourself.

For example, if your goal is financial success, your success may be defined by the possessions you purchase when you receive your money. Instead of writing down, "I want a new car," you would actually place a picture of the make, model, and color of your dream car on a poster board or in a notebook. In the earlier example, Stephanie cut out pictures from health and fitness magazines that were of women she wanted her body image to match.

Perhaps, you wish to own a new home. Place a picture of the home you wish to own or a copy of a blueprint on the poster board or paper. Continue in this fashion with all of your listed goals. The key is finding pictures that will reflect you already in possession of your desired goals. Just as writing down goals will help you crystallize success in your mind, so will visualizing through your image book or treasure map. Only you can control the images feeding your brain.

Most people find it difficult to visualize using their mind. You will be successful by visualizing over and over again. Repetition will win the battle for you. Think of all of the advertisements you see on television, direct mail, and in magazines. Why will a company spend millions of dollars in television advertisements to sell a $2.00 hamburger? They spend that kind of money because they know, that by giving you images of that hamburger, and by repeating that image many, many, times, they can change your eating behavior, forever!

Marketing studies have shown that people will buy just about anything, if they are shown that image enough times. For one person that may be just one or two viewings or "impressions." For another person, it may be one thousand impressions. How many impressions will it take for you to achieve your goal? View your image book or treasure map often and you will be achieving your goals before you know it. Repetition always wins.

After you are finished creating your image book or treasure map, place it on a wall or by your desk and look at it each day. Study it. As you concentrate on these visual images of what you want, your subconscious mind is working overtime to help you achieve your goals.

Your imagination is so powerful that you will start achieving these goals faster than you could ever imagine. You may find after time that some of the pictures aren't really goals anymore, so replace them with new goals. After a session of practicing your self-hypnosis, begin to recreate you image book. You will be surprised of the insights a session of self-hypnosis will give you.

Each day when you get up in the morning and before you go to bed at night, pass your image book or treasure map, and study each of the pictures. Allow your subconscious servant to do its work.

There are many magazines with colorful pictures to cut out and positive statements, (usually in the advertisements for products). Money Magazine, Kiplinger Magazine, The Wall Street Journal, have great financial goal pictures and copy. Health and Fitness magazines have great pictures of how you may want to look after you have gained or lost a certain amount of weight. Let you imagination be your guide. You will be in the hands of the best guide available!

After you have cut out the pictures, glue or paste them on your poster board. Look at them each every day. Cut out pictures when you don't want that goal anymore and replace them with new ones. When you achieve your goal, file it or place it in a prominent place to remind you of the power of your mind. Remember that you are the best hypnotist in the entire world, and also the best goal achiever you will ever meet!

Congratulations on your success.

Workshop

Activity 1 - My List of Goals

Write down a list of goals. List your main goals then less important ones. Make sure you include the goals that were important to you and you wrote down earlier. No goal is too large or too small. Your powerful subconscious mind is a powerful, goal-achieving machine. As you write down the goals and as you review them at a later date, see yourself in possession of the goals. See yourself enjoying the results of your hard work and dedication.

1.

2.

3.

4.

5.

6.

7.

8

9.

10.

11.

12.

13.

14.

15.

16.

113

17.

18.

19.

20.

Activity 2 - Create Your Image Book or Treasure Map

Collect all the newspapers, magazines and photographs you can find. Cut out pictures and headlines that most represent the goals you have listed in Activity 1. Take colored paper or poster board and paste or tape the pictures and headlines all over it. If you have more than one picture or representation for each goal that is fine. Your subconscious is a goal-achieving machine. It will enjoy achieving everything you give it. In addition, place a few of your main goal pictures and headlines below. Look at these pictures and headlines every time you open this book.

Activity 3 - Self-hypnosis Forum

Go on-line to the Self-hypnosis Forum, at http://www.wayneperkins.net and see what others are saying about their image books or treasure maps. Interact with others from around the country and around the world.

Summary

In Chapter 9, you learned two methods in achieving all of your goals. Make sure you write down what you want in life. If you can't write it down, you can't do it.

You also learned how to create an image book or treasure map. Picture yourself with these successful images. They will enhance your self-hypnosis improvement plan

Chapter 10 Perkins' Goal Achievement Program
Robert

Robert lost his two little girls. His ex-wife took them to a state across the country. She enrolled them in school and cut them off from their Dad. She was bitter after a divorce and wanted to punish Robert by making it impossible for him to see his precious children. Robert was losing sleep and needed self-hypnosis to help get some rest.

He decided to create and participate in a Success Support Group that was started by a church nearby. Here, he could ask for some moral support in achieving his goal of getting the court system to award him custody of his children. He met with 4 other people. After telling them this story, Robert asked that each of the four people hold in their thoughts the Court rule what was best for his two little girls. For three weeks of meeting with his newly found Success Support Group, Robert asked for this help and support in this challenge.

One week later the Court ordered his ex-wife to allow joint custody involving the return of the little girls to their Dad for two weeks. At the time this book was written, it looked very favorable that Robert would get full custody of the children as their Mother said she was not interested in raising them.

Objectives of Chapter 10

During this lesson you will learn how to create and participate in a success support group and achieve positive results just like Robert. You will learn the importance of becoming a "mentor," and then learn how to integrate those techniques through your self-hypnosis program.

Let's begin!

Create And Participate In A Success Support Group

What is a *success support group*? A success support group is a group of two or more people, dedicated in helping each other achieve goals. Usually 3 to 5 people work really well together. The purpose of the group is to support each other emotionally, while striving for success. This group may begin as a group of friends, or a group of complete strangers.

I prefer strangers. Have you ever noticed how you may relate to a complete stranger better than a family member or friend? I personally believe that sometimes we have other competitive issues with relatives and friends that we don't have with complete strangers. Your success will not make them feel jealous. In fact, they may feel by supporting you they helped create your success. With a stranger, there is no reward for them if you achieve. There is also no reward for them if you fail.

Here is how the Success Support Group works. You find through your church, place of work or another social setting 3 or 4 people whom would like to improve and achieve their personal goals much quicker. Other support group recruits may be found through Internet Chat or special interest Web Boards. One of the most successful success support groups I know of has been going on for almost 20 years. This group rarely sees each other face to face. They hold meetings via long distance telephone conference calls. Some Internet sites will allow you to hold your success support group for free via their Internet chat and Web board features. You will find some great ones listed in the appendix of this book. The Internet resources work well, especially for long distance, out of state, or out of the country support groups.

Once you have identified your group, find a time and a place that is convenient for your group to meet each week. I personally find that a once a week meeting keeps issues fresh and still gives enough time to work and complete short-term goals. Long-term goals can be accomplished by working on several related, short-term goals.

The meeting starts off with one person reading off the goals that they have for the coming week. They may include long term goals that they are working on as well. Usually long-term goals have many steps that can be monitored along the way at a forum like this one. After the first person has finished reading his goals, another member of the group will repeat back the first goal to him and express how he/she believes the goal achiever will reach that objective this week. An important feature of the Success Support Group is the fact that as a supporter, you do not try to offer unsolicited advice to solve the problem for the goal achiever. You do not want to diffuse the issue or take power away from the person seeking support. Let the person state the problem and then give unconditional support. If the person really wants you to help directly, they will ask you for it.

The Success Support Group dialog will go something like this. Even though in real life each person will have four or five goals to address. I will give you an example of the group dialog, limiting each member to just one objective.

Support Member #1

Support Group Member #1: "My goal this week is to exercise 3 times."

Support Group Member #2: " I see you having all the motivation you need to complete exercise 3 times this week."

Support Group Member #3: "Member #1, I envision you exercising, getting your heart rate up and feeling good about the process." "You will feel a sense of achievement and accomplishment."

Support Group Member #4: " I too am excited about the fact that you wish to exercise three times this week." "You will feel so much better when you come back here next week and tell us about your completion of the exercises."

Support Member #2

Support Group Member #2: "My goal is to look for a new job." "I want a job that will pay me what I feel I'm worth." "I want a job that will give me a great deal of personal satisfaction."

Support Member #1: "I think that it is great that you are trying to better yourself." "It shows you have a great deal of self-confidence and self-love." "I see you getting solid interviews this week."

Support Group Member #3: "I envision you rapidly getting into the career of your dreams." "People want to offer you an exciting job that will carry a great deal of personal satisfaction along with a great deal of money."

Support Group Member #4: "I have to agree with the others." "All this week I am going to envision you getting the proper direction and motivation to find your new career with exciting challenges that will bring you money and satisfaction."

Once everyone has given their goals to the group and in turn, received verbal reaffirming of the expectation to achieve, the group is finished for the week. After a while, you may relate more and more very personal goals to the group and they will feel comfortable relating their innermost goals to you. Some of the goals that you may discuss will be concerning health, money, career, education, family and relationships. You can work on short-term goals and long-term goals at the same time.

This is a great way to achieve success. Working with new people, who have no reason to question your abilities or feel jealous about your success, is a great way to explore new goals and to forge ahead, toward successful completion of you current goals. It is a real confidence booster to look in strangers' eyes and see them on fire with enthusiasm. They are reflecting the enthusiasm in your eyes.

Nothing in life is more powerful than that.

I have participated in several Success Support Groups over the years and have started several others. I wish you could see how these groups become so important in the lives of the participants. The Success Support Group becomes one of the most important and satisfying parts of the goal achiever's life.

I hope it becomes an important part of your life.

Mr. Heffron

The year I was graduating from high school, I had an urge to learn a musical instrument. At the time, several entertainers were recording hit songs using brass instruments. I wanted to play Trumpet just like Al Hirt from New Orleans. My younger sister, who was going to Algonquin Junior High School in Algonquin, Illinois, said she had a great band instructor who offers private lessons. His primary instrument in College was the Trumpet. He put himself through school playing in Jazz Bands and Wedding Bands. His name was Mr. Heffron.

I gave Mr. Heffron a call.

Unlike many of the teachers I had in high school, this man was very dedicated.

Many of my other teachers were not. For example: I had one teacher that couldn't give me help because he was a football coach and couldn't help me during the fall football season. When the spring school semester started, the same teacher couldn't help me because he was moonlighting, selling insurance policies to students.

Mr. Heffron was different. He was young and enthusiastic about music and enthusiastic about teaching it to others. He drove twenty miles out of this way to my home to deliver my lesson. He only charged me $2.00, which barely covered the gas of his 1964 Corvair. He also gave me reams of his favorite sheet music for free. This was music he loved and wanted to share with the world.

He became my Mentor.

I ended up quitting my lessons after about nine months. I got drafted into the Army, and went overseas. I lost track of Mr. Heffron. When I was discharged from the Army, two years later,

I found out that Mr. Heffron was the Band Director for Dundee High School in Carpentersville, Illinois. This was the very school that I graduated from three years earlier! He created the Dundee Scots Marching Band. The Dundee Scots were a competition high school band that dressed in kilts and played traditional instruments along with bagpipes.
They were sensational!
The Dundee Scots were invited to parades all over the United States and competed and won many competitions across the country. Mr. Heffron's teaching style and leadership ability created exciting groups of motivated students and chaperones, to guide the students to successful and rewarding lives. He became a mentor for many students.

I graduated with a degree in Business Education from Northern Illinois University and taught three years at Elgin High School in Elgin, Illinois. I have taught people how to hypnotize themselves and how to hypnotize others for over 20 years. Many of my students learned how to reduce stress and pain in their lives. Many of these people learned how to achieve many exciting goals, just like yours.

Fill out the registration form located in the appendix of this book. Send it to me, and receive your certificate for a free, self-hypnosis workshop. After the free workshop, don't thank me. Thank the memory of my Mentor...Mr. Heffron.

Step 5: Become A Mentor

Are you a mentor? Is there someone in your life that looks up to you? Has there ever been a younger brother or sister, or friend that thought of you as the most important person on the planet?

Everyone is a mentor. Sometimes, however, you have no idea of the person or persons are who you are inspiring on a day to day basis. We go through life unaware that we make a difference in the world. Its time that you made a concerted effort to realize how your life brings meaning to others. Contact school counselors, civic, church groups, and governmental agencies to see if you can locate people or groups that need mentoring. Find someone you can help.

Napoleon Hill, in his book *Think And Grow Rich*, recalls a quote by the motivational speaker, Earl Nightingale. The quote is "The fastest way to reach your goal, is to help someone else, achieve theirs."

Mr. Heffron helped me and a lot of others reach their goals. He was a man of great personal integrity and personal success. By affecting others in such a positive way, he achieved his personal goals and his students achieved theirs. When that someone else respects you for your achievements in the area of academics, sports, music, art, or the medical field, they will accept your suggestions much more readily than from anyone else.

The suggestions you give are called *prestige suggestions*. Prestige suggestions are accepted as fact by the subconscious mind of your student or mentee. As these suggestions are accepted as fact by the subconscious mind they set up behavior patterns that may affect your student for a lifetime! Parents, teachers, law enforcement officials, movie stars, judges, hypnotists, and medical doctors are just some of the people that offer prestige suggestions in your life. Imagine how effective you will be mentoring an individual who accepts you and your beliefs as readily as the suggestions you receive from the *prestige* group.

Become a Mentor.

Integrating Goal Achievement with Self-hypnosis

How do you integrate the 5 step goal achievement plan with you self-hypnosis training? Since hypnosis is a goal achieving mechanism in itself, we find that it is rather easy to integrate the process. The best way to learn is by doing. You know deep down how to integrate the two. Offering yourself pre-hypnotic suggestions, creating visualization where you see yourself achieving these goals, and then a suggestion that after your self-hypnotic session, you will begin to work on the five-step program.

Workshop

Activity 1 - Record Your Ideas

Think about the 5-Step Goal Achievement Program. Make a list below of suggestions you can give yourself that will help you integrate the 5-Steps into your everyday life. Note your suggestions that coincide with each step.

1. Bury the Dead

2. Write it Down

3. Create an Image Book or Treasure Map

4. Create and Participate in a Success Support Group

5. Become a Mentor

Activity 2 - Become A Mentor

Think about all of your accomplishments and achievements in your personal life. Begin with your very first memory in life. In the space below, fill in the positive accomplishments as you remember them. No accomplishment is too small or insignificant. You never know how that achievement will be received from others, and how powerful a force it will become in their lives.

After you have completed all of the blanks, think of people you know that you may be able to help based on any of these achievements. If you can't think of specific people, what children's' groups, organizations or associations would benefit by your talents in these areas? List them next to the categories.

Subjects in school

Athletics

Music or Art

Consulting

Job Skills

Hobby Skills

Household Skills

Child Rearing Skills

Negotiating Skills

Careers

Religion and/or Philosophy

Games

Outdoor Skills

Other

Activity 3 - Self-hypnosis Forum

Follow the link at http://www.wayneperkins.net and enter the Self-hypnosis Forum. Read and contribute to the postings there. What new ideas can you use from others living around the globe?

Summary

You are rapidly achieving your goals. By integrating the goal achievement techniques you mastered over the last three chapters and integrating them into your success plan, you are developing methods that will help you achieve all of your goals for years to come. Use this book every time you go after a new goal. Make copies of the activities located in the appendix of this book. You will be successful each and every time you execute your success program.

I wish you the best in your success. You have already achieved some of your goals. There is still more in life to do.

Let's achieve some more.

Chapter 11 Using the Laws of Suggestion The Show...

Let's go back in time.

Return with me to my first college stage performance in 1977. You will be sitting in the audience. Picture yourself sitting in a large circular college activity center, located at Loras College in Dubuque, Iowa. It is a Saturday night and there are about 7000 people in attendance. There are the students, and faculty of Loras College as well as students from other schools located nearby. As you look up on the elevated stage you notice just one-man present and 18 empty, metal folding chairs located behind him. You wonder as you look up on stage, "Who is going to volunteer to be put in the hypnotic trance? Once they are in that hypnotic trance, what are they going to do?"

The stage hypnotist is now asking the entire audience to participate in a live experiment involving *suggestion*, the basis of *hypnotism*. The stage hypnotist, Wayne F. Perkins, raises his arms to get your attention and says: "Here is an experiment in suggestion you all can participate in right from your chair located in the audience." He continues: "Close your eyes. Take three slow deep breaths. Each time you inhale, breathe in life sustaining oxygen. Each time you exhale, push all of the tension completely out of your lungs. Now open your eyes and focus your attention at me, here on stage."

The stage hypnotist is now holding a large, yellow lemon in his left hand. He is holding it high in the air for everyone to see. Wayne continues: "Before you, I hold a large, sour, bitter, juicy, yellow lemon. It is such a sour, bitter juicy, yellow, lemon. Now a take a knife out of my pocket and I cut into this sour, bitter, juicy, yellow, lemon. As I cut into the lemons some of the sour, bitter, juice drops to the floor. Now, I take the sour, bitter, juicy, yellow, lemon to my mouth. I begin to suck on this sour, bitter, juice." Wayne adds: "Notice how your mouths tend to fill with saliva." You have experienced hypnotic suggestion."

Objectives of Chapter 11

In this chapter, you will learn some very important hypnotism theory. In most hypnotism books you find these principles located in the first few chapters. I feel strongly that by having you develop your own techniques based on the limited theory I presented in chapters one and two, you will have success and goal achievement before you are presented with more advanced theory.

Since all hypnosis is self-hypnosis, your success is directed by the *gut feeling* you have in applying my text up until now. By presenting other theories relating to self-hypnosis, you will be able to refine your techniques and be able to diagnose any problems in your self-hypnosis *style*.

Your success in achievement is important to me. If anything in this or the previous chapters are unclear, please e-mail me at: wayne@wayneperkins.net or participate in the Self-hypnosis Forum located at: http://www.wayneperkins.net where other students and hypnotherapists will help you.

Let's begin!

What Is Suggestion?

Suggestions are words and/or ideas that cause our body to react physically. For example, if you smell you favorite dish cooking, your salivary glands will secret. You will begin to water at the mouth as your body anticipates tasting and breaking down the foods you only smell at the moment. If someone tells you that you look sick, you may begin to feel sick. Even if you were feeling great at the time, enough of those you-look-sick suggestions may cause physical illness in your body. If someone that you admire tells you how great a song is, you may listen and feel the same way. Again, this may happen even if it isn't the type of music you would normally listen to. Can you think of a time when this happened to you?

Suggestions don't always apply to hypnosis in the classic sense. Suggestions also refer to subtle influences or direct influences one person exhibits over another person. When you raise your voice in anger and direct it toward your spouse or your children, you cause their behavior to change (at least temporarily). When you give a person a reward, "Hey, I will give you $20.00 if you quack like a duck," some people for $20.00 would quack like a duck. When you are at a sporting event are you more likely to stand up and yell for your team, if everyone at the game is participating than if you are watching the game by yourself at home? This would be an example of a subtle suggestion. Other people are helping you temporarily, change your behavior.

There are many types of suggestions that affect human behavior.

Direct suggestions are statements to encourage you to act automatically and immediately. When I was in the Army, if my drill sergeant would shout at me to duck, I would duck without question. The penalty of looking around instead of ducking may be injury or death. Even though I have been out of the Army for over 30 years, if someone were to stand behind me and shout, "Duck!" I would be the first to unquestionably hit the ground!

Indirect suggestions are much subtler. Sometimes you are unaware that they are even happening at the time. For example, if a person in your workplace or classroom yawns, you may yawn as well. If a stranger comes up to you and smiles, you may automatically smile at the stranger. Shaking your head no, or shaking your fist at someone, will also get an unconscious response.

In a previous chapter, I discussed *prestige suggestions*. These are suggestions we accept as fact because we truly believe in the person giving the suggestions. A famous clergy person is telling you how great you are, a teacher is telling you that you are a remarkable student, a famous entertainer is complimenting you on your music or art skills. All of these suggestions are

131

accepted into your subconscious mind as prestige suggestions.

Listening to music or looking at fine art to get into a certain mood, are examples of *non-prestige suggestions*. Certain music may suggest dance, laughter, sorrow, relaxation, etc. Certain pieces of art also suggest feelings that the subconscious mind begins to act upon. Are may have a calming effect or one which stimulates your creativity.

When your body seems to react automatically to these suggestions, the hypnotic condition is produced.

What Is Critical Thought?

What is critical thought? Why is it important? When someone commands you by saying, "Sit down," you may first evaluate the situation. You may think, why should I sit down? Why is the person commanding me to sit down without explanation? What do I have to gain by following this person's instructions? You may decide that you don't want to sit down and you may tell the person, that you prefer to stand.

Critical thoughts are those thoughts that are evaluating the other person's commands or suggestions, before we take action. When you are deeply hypnotized, and someone says, "Sit down," you just sit down immediately. Your body reacts as if it had a mind of its own. You respond very quickly and decisively to the command. The suggestion bypasses the *critical thought* part of our mind.

When you use self-hypnosis, attempt to bypass critical thought. If you are a smoker who desires to become a non-smoker, tell yourself that you ARE a nonsmoker and that each day you practice more and more that you ARE a nonsmoker. If you find that as you are giving yourself this suggestion, you are asking yourself questions like, "why should I? Why am I doing this? What do I have to gain? Stop for a moment and take yourself back to breathing deeply and relaxing. Think of pleasing surroundings, music, art, pleasant smells, etc. Soon a more positive mood will present itself and healing will take place. You will be back on track.

Only, after you relax and clear your mind, do you go back and start on your positive prescription, as your subconscious mind becomes open to suggestion.

Remember when you were a child. Your parents may have mentioned that Santa Claus was going to bring you presents. The thought of getting presents was so appealing to your imagination that you accepted it as fact. Your parents hypnotized you. When you became 7 or 8 years of age, you thought more and more critically. You had more experiences to draw upon and you become more opinionated than when you heard about Santa Claus for the first time. Think more and more as a young child does when you hypnotize yourself. Remember when you were small ALL things were possible. It's only after adult life has beaten you over the head that you remain in a critical mode of thinking.

Think as a child and achieve all things in life.

Making the Law of Reverse Effect Work For You

What is the law of reversed effect? The law of reversed effect was first written about by the great French philosopher, Emile Coue', who stated, "the harder you try to do something, the harder it becomes."

Think about it. Have you ever attempted to do well in one of your studies in school, or in learning a skill in sports, only to fail after you have "tried" it several times? We teach ourselves to "try harder." We try harder only to fail. This is how the law of reversed effect works. The word "try" implies doubt in your abilities. Whenever you are in a situation or you are attempting to achieve a goal, don't "try" to do it. Relax and envision yourself achieving the goal, or overcoming the situation. See yourself very clearly in your mind's eye, already in possession of your goal. If you are starting a new task, relax and feel confident that you have everything you need to achieve success.

133

Relax, let go, and achieve success. Success will come to you, once you let your guard down and allow it to enter your life.

Let's Hypnotize Ourselves

This time we are going to use an induction that will include *convincers*. Convincers are exercises that allow you to *feel* hypnotized. These are exercises that test if you have bypassed your critical thought. They also use Emile Coue's *law of reversed effect*.

Here is how it works. As you progress through the eyes closed induction, I present, I will give an exercise that will allow you to imagine your eyelids are fastened down so tightly that you cannot open your eyes when *you try as hard as you can*. When you find that your imagination has fastened your eyelids together temporarily, your subconscious mind will open much faster and become more receptive to your personal prescription. As your critical thought becomes bypassed, you will find yourself going deeper into this wonderful state of mind. I will insert 3 critical thought exercises. Test yourself, than move on deeper into hypnosis. You will always know that you can open your eyes at anytime, however as you pretend that your imagination is causing this to happen, critical thought is being bypassed and you really are sinking down deeper into this wonderful state.

Let's begin.

Get your tape recorder ready and prepare to record this exercise using your own voice.

BEGIN INDUCTION

Sit up in your favorite chair, or lie down on your couch or bed and begin to relax. You may find that after the weeks we have been doing these exercises, that already your eyelids want to close down and allow you to feel that familiar feeling of deep and perfect relaxation. (Pause)

Now close your eyes and take three deep breaths. (Pause)

As you exhale, let all of the tension leave your lungs. (Pause)

You are going, deep, deep, and deep into hypnosis. (Pause)

Nothing will awaken you; nothing will disturb you as you relax very, very deeply. (Pause)

Your mind is keenly alert and aware, as your body is relaxing deeply. (Pause)

Each and every deep breath is assisting you in relaxing deeply, each and every sound that you hear is assisting you in relaxing deeply. (Pause)

You are gaining more and more control over the subconscious part of your mind. (Pause)

Now picture yourself walking up to an elevator. (Pause)

You are on the tenth floor and the elevator will take you on a relaxing ride down to the first floor. (Pause)

I will count at the same time from 10 down to 1. As I begin counting, think about the elevator ride going form the 10th floor down to the first floor. (Pause)

As you picture yourself taking the slow, relaxing, elevator ride down to the first floor, you will become more relaxed than ever before. (Pause)

All right, 10 you are getting into the elevator and the door is shutting behind you. (Pause)

9, you are going deeper and sounder into this relaxing feeling of hypnosis. (Pause)

8, deeper and sounder than ever before, as

the elevator travels downward. (Pause)

7, all of your body is relaxing as you drift off toward hypnosis. (Pause)

6, breathing deeply and relaxing deeply (Pause)

5, the elevator is nearing the fifth floor and you feel as if you are lighter than air, as you drift peacefully toward sleep and relaxation. (Pause)

4, deeper, sounder and more perfectly, relaxed. (Pause)

3, every muscle and fiber is totally and completely, relaxed. (Pause)

2, you are almost at your destination. (Pause)

1, you are on the ground floor, you are deeply and completely, relaxed. (Pause)

Think about relaxing the muscles around your eyelids. In a moment your eyelids will be stuck together, tightly. They will be stuck together so tightly that you will test them and find that they are stuck together tightly. So tightly stuck together, that it will be impossible for you to open your eyelids no matter how hard you try. (Pause)

Think about relaxing those muscles around your eyelids. Stick those eyelids so tightly together that you absolutely cannot open your eyes no matter how hard you try. Try as hard as you can to open your eyes. Try two or three times. (Pause)

Now forget about your eyes and go deeper and sounder into this pleasant state of mind. Keep your eyes closed down and relax deeper than ever before. (Pause)

Now, pretend that either your left leg or your right leg is filled with sand and getting very, very heavy. (Pause)

Your leg is becoming so heavy that you will not be able to lift it, now matter how hard you try. Try as hard as you can to lift that heavy leg. Try once or twice. (Pause)

Now forget about your leg, and as you do, you are going deeper and deeper into this pleasant state of hypnosis. (Pause)

Now as you relax in hypnosis, imagine that one of your arms is filled with helium gas. Picture your arm being filled with helium gas, and as your arm fills with helium gas it begins to rise up from your side or from your lap. (Pause)

Your arm is so light, it is lighter than air and is rising up in the air. (Pause)

As your arm rises in the air, you are going deeper, and deeper into this deep state of hypnosis. (Pause)

Your mind is alert and aware as your body is relaxing soundly, and perfectly. (Pause)

Now imagine letting all the helium gas out of your arm and letting your arm fall back into your lap, or by your side. (Pause)

As your arm falls back into your lap or by your side, you are going deeper and deeper into hypnosis. (Pause)

Your mind is keenly alert and aware, as your body relaxes perfectly and completely. (Pause)

In a moment you will prepare to emerge from this wonderful state of hypnosis. (Pause)

You will find that after you emerge from hypnosis that all of your regular sensations return to your body. Your mind will be rested, refreshed and ready to move on to more exciting things in your life. As you use this and the other exercises I have given you during the past 11 chapters, you will find yourself achieving your goals much quicker than ever before. You are calm and confident and filled with the self-satisfaction of becoming the master of your mind and master of your destiny. (Pause)

At the count of five you will be wide-awake, alert, rested, refreshed and all sensation will come back to your body. (Pause)

Okay, One, get ready, to return. Two, your breathing is speeding up a little bit as you move toward the conscious state. Three get ready now. Four, Five, wide awake, alert, and feeling good in every way!

END INDUCTION

How do you feel? Wasn't that fun? Did you enjoy the "convincers?" Did you see and hear the word "try" to practice the law of reversed effect?

The next time you watch a stage hypnotist, notice how he or she employs the law of reversed effect and uses convincers to deepen the effect of the hypnosis on stage.

Workshop

Activity 1 - Evaluation of the **Convincer Induction**

Record your reactions and thoughts to this exercise by answering the following questions.

1. What was the first thing you thought about as you finished the exercise?

.

2. How did you feel during the exercise?

3. How do you feel now?

4. Did you have any unusual sensations as you were listening to your voice?

5. List anything that you feel was "memorable" during the exercise.

Activity 2 - Compare Your Experience With Others

Fire up your computer and go to my website located at:

http://www.wayneperkins.net

Compare your experience with others from around the world.

Summary

In Chapter 11, you learned some basic hypnotism theory. You successfully experienced that theory in action with the hypnotic "Convincer Induction." You are now ready for some great experiences in using the power of your own mind!

You now have learned a wonderful skill. You have mastered the exercises and are achieving your goals.

Part 2 of this book includes more hypnosis theory, the history of hypnosis, and many Internet resources that will help you achieve all of your goals.

I wish you success.

Part 2

Hypnosis Resources

Hypnosis History

Hypnosis Theory

Chapter 12 Using Hypnosis and Self-improvement Resources

Your life, like this book, is a work in progress. Use the techniques learned in Chapter's 1-11, to help you achieve your goals. In addition to the skills learned earlier, you have many self-hypnosis and goal achievement resources available with just a small amount of research. Many of these resources are available through the Internet at no cost to you. Your investment in this book and your confidence in your own abilities, have guaranteed your success. Remember that repetition of the activities presented will ultimately bring positive results.

Objectives of Chapter 12

The objectives of Chapter 12 are to acquaint you with the additional services you will receive by your purchase of this book, and my on-going strategy to help you achieve all of your goals in the future.

"My mission in life is to help you achieve your mission in life.

Key Points to Remember

Always remember that repetition of the activities and exercises you learned in this book will help your mind "rewire" its circuits and create new and positive habit patterns. Here are some additional Key Points to always remember:

1.   Label your recorded tapes and remember which ones work best for you.

2.   Hypnotize yourself at approximately the same time each day. However, if your schedule cannot accommodate,

try a new routine. Go and make the new routine work. You are in charge of your success.

3. If you usually lie down during self-hypnosis and find yourself falling asleep before you are through with the assignment, sit up in a less comfortable chair.

4. Don't worry about the length of the induction. If you need to shorten it, fine. Think about television commercials. They are hypnotic, short and sweet. It's the repetition that changes your habit patterns and causes you to buy.

5. Think about images or graphics that you can always add to your self-hypnosis plan.

6. Create and work your own prescription. Always use positive words and images.

7. Think about your senses. Focus on your favorite sense while you are creating and using your hypnotic inductions.

8. Always forgive others. By forgiving others, you will forgive yourself and remove obstacles to success.

9. When you don't feel like using self-hypnosis, use Perkins' 5-Step Goal Achievement Program.

10. Never give up! Never, never, never give up! Your success will inspire others!

The Self-hypnosis Forum

What is the Self-hypnosis Forum and why is it important? Where is it located? The Self-hypnosis Forum is a computer "message board" located on the Hypnotism Education Website at http://www.wayneperkins.net

The Forum allows you to post questions and the Internet, that hundreds, even thousands of students can view and respond to. Hypnotists and hypnotherapists from all over the world have access to it as well. Many experiences may be shared and many friends made at the same time. Once you mail back the *How to Hypnotize Yourself Without Losing Your Mind Registration*

Form, you will be assigned an Internet address where you can enter the Self-hypnosis Forum. This is a powerful self-help system that taps into thousands of creative and helpful minds... yours included.

Self-hypnosis Chat

The Self-hypnosis Chat Service is similar to the Self-hypnosis Forum in that you may discuss issues and converse with students and hypnotherapists from around the world. However, you will be able to converse on-line and in *real-time*. Real-time means the communicants will all be logged on the Self-hypnosis Chat Service at the same time. You will be able to talk through your fingers and your keyboard, to many people at the same time. Short workshops and question/answer periods will be arranged at a variety of times to accommodate the different time zones throughout the world.

Again, once you register with me by filling out the registration form located in the appendix of this book, you will receive further instructions on how to use the Self-hypnosis Chat Service. The service is free for you.

You will love it! It's a great way to share with others, your successes using self-hypnosis. Also you will see people offer many questions regarding the topics of hypnotism and self-improvement. You may discover and create Success Support Groups from people participating in the Self-hypnosis Forum and the Self-hypnosis Chat Service.

Feel free to join in the worldwide conversation!

The Complete Hypnosis Bookstore

In the beginning, when I wanted information on hypnosis and self-hypnosis, I had to rely on the local library. I read the only three books I could find there over. I read each book, many, many times. I practically memorized them. It was always hard to find books and tapes on the subject of hypnosis and self-hypnosis. Now, you and I have access to over 7000 books and tapes on hypnosis! Everything you ever wanted to know about hypnosis and the hundreds of applications of hypnosis can be found at the Hypnosis Bookstore. Not only will you find the book you want, but also you will save between 10% and 30% off of suggested retail pricing on every purchase.

The Hypnosis Bookstore is located on my Hypnotism Education Website at the following Internet address:
http://www.wayneperkins.net/hypnosis/books.html
A description of several hypnosis books is located there plus a powerful search engine that will help you find any book in print at a fantastic discount. Books may be purchased and shipped anywhere in the world. I am committed to offering you the latest and most complete library of hypnosis books and tapes available anywhere. Save the above Internet Hypnosis Bookstore address as one of your favorites! Once you see how easy it is to use the search box located on the site, you will be purchasing all of your books and music at discount prices for years to come. Complete reviews, pictures, and stories about the authors are found here as well.

I am committed to your personal achievement and success!

The Goal Achievement Newsletter

The Goal Achievement Newsletter is a short newsletter delivered by e-mail, designed to focus on how you can achieve all of your goals at a much greater rate. Some of the goal setting and goal achieving techniques mentioned in this book will be included, as well as success stories from people using those techniques and other techniques they find more helpful. Please send me your personal success story. Other people from around the world would love to be inspired by your achievements! Since the newsletter schedule is based on my busy schedule, it is delivered on a rather random basis. However, it is delivered around 4 or 5 times per year.

Once you send in your registration form, located in the book appendix, you will start receiving your Goal Achievement Newsletter. You will receive the free newsletter for as long as you want it. You may delete or unsubscribe at any time.

Seminars and Workshops

I present many seminars and workshops in the Southwestern United States. Most of them are held in Arizona and California. However, I do have full day Self-hypnosis Workshops, and Past Life Regression, in many major cities throughout the United States. You will be sent my updated Workshop Schedule with your registration information.

After you send in your registration form, you will receive FREE admission for my full-day, *How To Hypnotize Yourself, Without Losing Your Mind: Workshop*. There you will be able to share your techniques with others working on achieving all of their goals. You will also receive major discounts on other workshops and seminars I present in Arizona, and throughout the United States.

My Books, Tapes and Other Learning Opportunities

Thank you for purchasing my book.

You made an excellent decision. You will receive discounts on any tapes, books, and other learning opportunities, as I develop them. As the Internet changes and evolves, I will change and evolve too, in order to give you new learning opportunities and experiences. Learning can become candy to the brain. I want more and more of that candy. How about you?

Updated Versions of This Book

This book was created electronically in an *on-demand* mode. What this means is that as new revisions of this book come out, you do not have to purchase another book.

Once you have sent in the registration you will be given an address on the Internet where additional revisions of the book will be located. When I find a new and exciting technique that will help you achieve your goals, you will be able to download the new page or pages that are changed.

If I add or change a chapter in this book or give additional case histories, you again will find them at a private Internet address. You may periodically look at my site address to view or print out the changes or wait until you are notified by e-mail or snail-mail when those changes are available. The fact that your book may change and yet, you only have one manufactured copy will help our environment. There will be none of my "older book versions" clogging landfills around the world.

Summary

You and your life are a work in progress.

Remember that all of your problems won't be solved and your goals achieved overnight. With daily practice of the self-hypnosis skills you learned in the "How To Hypnotize Yourself Without Losing Your Mind," you will have everything you need to achieve success.

You always had and will always have everything you need to achieve what you want in life. Sometimes, you only need to be reminded how wonderful and powerful you are.

Thank you for giving me your trust. I am honored that you read this book and look forward in helping you achieve all of your goals in the future.

Please e-mail me your accomplishments. I will be interested in your accomplishments for years to come! If you want to share your accomplishments with the world, send me your story and I will select the best ones to publish in my updates, the Hypnotism Education Website, and the Goal Achievement Newsletter.

And always remember...

"My mission in life is to help you achieve your mission in life."

--Wayne F. Perkins, Certified Clinical Hypnotherapist

Chapter 13 The History Of Hypnosis

Where did hypnosis come from? Who invented it? How was it used?

Objectives Chapter 13

The objectives of this chapter are for you to become aware of the long history of hypnosis.

You also should be able to identify some of the key figures in the introduction of hypnosis in medical science.

In the Beginning

Hypnosis has been around a long time in history. Hieroglyphics from the Tomb of Isis in ancient Egypt shows worshipers experiencing hypnotic sleep. In fact, in ancient Egypt the correct term is "curing sleep." A priest or ruler placed people in the condition and illnesses were treated by suggestion. In ancient Greece statues depict trance like states. The statues were created over 2,000 years ago.

Primitive societies used hypnotic phenomena throughout the ages for physical and spiritual benefits. Tribal drums and ritualistic dances have been a part of many societies in Africa and South America. Kings of middle age Europe would touch commoners with remarkable results. Priests and ministers would use a laying-on of hands to affect changes in their church members.

Mesmer

Frederick (Franz) Anton Mesmer wrote an important thesis

149

titled *The Influence of the Stars and Planets as Curative Powers*, in 1773. This work claimed that the planets, stars and the moon affected humans through *animal magnetism*. Animal magnetism refers to an invisible energy fluid that runs through every human being. Mesmer went on to say that the placement of magnets around a person who is diseased will help improve the flow of the healthy fluids, thus restoring the person back to health.

Mesmer practiced using this magnetism all over his native Austria as well as Western Europe. He treated cases of hysteria with magnets. Mesmer theorized the magnet cured with physical properties, interrupting the sick person's magnetic field. If a person became sick, he felt this simple act of passing a magnet over the person's body would restore him to perfect health.

This animal magnetism theory was confirmed in Mesmer's mind from his personal observation of Father Gassner, a Catholic Priest, who would heal people by using laying-on of hands. He would make numerous passes all over the subject's body. Mesmer studied Father Gassner very carefully and theorized that this magnetic fluid circulating in the body was affecting these changes. Forces from astral bodies affected this animal magnetism fluid.

There were four primary fluids of concern. These four fluids included blood, phlegm, yellow bile and black bile. Keeping these fluids in harmony was a major ingredient in good health. The theory of animal magnetism was sound at that time and coincided with Ben Franklin's discovery of electricity and recent advances in astronomy.

Mesmer moved to Paris in 1778 and invented *backquets*. These backquets were large iron pots that would hold many of his patients. He would line the backquets with iron filings and magnets. Patients would enter the bath, immerse themselves with water and leave cured of their ailments. Mesmer had a very high percentage of cures.

In 1784, the French Academy of Sciences, set up a commission to study Mesmer and set forth to find internationally famous scientists to investigate animal magnetism. International scientists: Ben Franklin, Lavoisier, and Dr. Guillotin, a chemist and inventor of the *guillotine*, were asked to study Mesmer and his techniques.

Mesmer took two large iron rods and touched these rods to several trees in the forest to *magnetize* them. His patients were asked to go into the forest and touch the magnetized trees. It was business as usual for Mesmer because many patients came back cured of their afflictions. However, patients were touching all the trees in the forest, not just the magnetized ones. Ben Franklin and the other scientists arrived at the conclusion that Mesmer was not healing the patients.

The patient was healing by using his own power. The patient's imagination was stimulated in such a way that would enable him to become completely healed!

This is exciting! This experiment helps demonstrate that all hypnosis is self-hypnosis. We all have the power to create positive change. All we have to do is to relax and focus.

Elliotson

Dr. John Elliotson was a professor of surgery at the University College in London, England. He is best known as the inventor of the stethoscope. John was a big supporter of Mesmer and used Mesmerism on many patients to reduce pain from surgery and for the treatment and cure of mental disorders.

Other surgeons at the college thought he was a quack so they condemned his practices. But they kept his stethoscope.

Braid

Dr. James Braid was a Scottish physician who lived from 1795-1860. Braid is sometimes called the *father of modern hypnosis*. He actually coined the term, *hypnosis*. He took it from the Greek word, *hypnos*, meaning *sleep*.

Once the term hypnosis caught on, Dr. Braid thought it over and theorized that the hypnotic subject is never really asleep. So he changed the word to *monoideism*. Monoideism means one word or one thought. Dr. Braid felt that the hypnotic subject was so focused on one thought or idea to the exclusion of all others that the trance like condition ensued. This is pretty much what all hypnotists believe today. The term monoideism never caught on. Hypnosis is here to stay!

Today

Today, hypnosis has many uses. Medical doctors and dentists, to help patients control pain are using it. Psychologists and Psychiatrists are using hypnosis to diagnose and treat many kinds of mental illnesses.

There are hypnotists and hypnotherapists that work with people to help them overcome bad habits and addictions. Helping people understand their past and helping them re-live past lives (past-life regression and past life therapy) are other very popular uses for hypnosis.

Now, using self-hypnosis to achieve your personal goals, is a popular and easy way to guarantee personal success.

...And you never lose your mind.

Workshop for Chapter 13

Activity 1 - Questions and Answers

Answer the following questions:
1. In your opinion, why are so many people afraid of hypnosis?

2. Who is the father of "hypnosis" and why do they call him that?

3. Where did the term "mesmerize" come from?

4. What is "animal magnetism"?

5. Who invented the "stethoscope?"

Activity 2 - The Self-hypnosis Forum

Go to the Self-hypnosis Forum located at: http://www.wayneperkins.net and read and post any information you desire regarding Chapter 13 The History of Hypnosis. Record any important information below.

Activity 3 - Your History

In the space below, tell me how you feel your own personal history will change as a result of using the self-hypnosis and powerful goal achievement techniques presented in this book? How will the histories of the lives that you touch, change as well?

Summary

You learned about some of the great people in hypnosis. You learned that this is not a new mental process. It has been going on since time was recorded. You are keeping it alive and making history right now!

Chapter 14 More Hypnosis Theory

Learning the psychological theory behind the hypnosis, you can form new insights and ideas, which may change your life.

I remember when I was a professional musician. I played by "gut feeling." I really didn't know much music "theory." I played guitar by ear and didn't read music. I formed a duo with a woman who was a very technical musician. As I learned more theory from her, I discovered my learning of intricate patterns in music became a lot easier. Now music began to make sense.

So it is with hypnosis. As you learn more hypnosis theory, you will increase your ability to succeed. You may enjoy using the theories or invent your own. As I said many times before, you are always the best hypnotist for yourself. Everything you need to be successful, you already possess.

Objectives of Chapter 14

The objectives of Chapter 14 are for you to understand some of the theory behind hypnosis and then apply this theory to your everyday life. Books will be listed in the bibliography located in the appendix, which will give you more theory and principles of hypnosis.

Let us begin!

Hypnosis Effects

Are there any side effects of hypnosis? Are any of these effects harmful?

There are some very interesting side effects of hypnosis. Some of these side effects may be construed as harmful.

Rapport

The first effect when a hypnotist is involved is the effect of increased *rapport*. As the subject or hypnotee is responding to the directions of the hypnotist a relationship begins on a very unique level. Just think about it. The hypnotist may be someone the subject has never met before, and the subject is going to trust the hypnotist with the most important part of his being. The subject is going to give the hypnotist control over his/her mind and body.

This is really an illusion of course. But, it happens just the same. As the subject allows more and more of this artificial control to be in the hands of the hypnotist, more and more amazing phenomena is produced by the hypnotee. This is why more and more sales organizations want their salesman to know basic hypnotic techniques. As rapport grows between hypnotist and subject, more control barriers are broken down. The two begin to think as one.

In a stage hypnosis presentation, the more the subject responds to the hypnotist's suggestions, the less likely the subject will be distracted by people talking or even shouting from the audience. The subject will seem to hone in on the sound of the hypnotist's voice. He/she will turn up the volume of the sound frequency of the hypnotist' voice and turn down the volume of all other sounds.

Rapport is the most common side effect of hypnosis.

Time Distortion

Time distortion is an interesting effect. Time distortion is the ability of the hypnotee to be able to accurately estimate time, expand time or contract time during the hypnosis experience.

Have you ever set your alarm clock for an important event only to wake up about 30 seconds before the alarm going off? The subconscious mind has an unbelievable way of estimating time when we are hypnotized or when we are asleep. If you are involved in a job that is very repetitive, such as running a production machine or working on an assembly line, you will experience the estimating time phenomenon many times in your workday.

If you are hypnotizing yourself, you can tell yourself as you close your eyes that you will awaken from hypnosis in two minutes and you will awaken in two minutes. Time distortion can be very helpful. You can expand time with hypnosis. This has already happened to you.

Did you ever have a bad day at work or school? Did you find the day seem a lot longer than a typical day at work or school? This is how time expands with hypnosis. You were so involved with the misery of your day. You then had a fear the day would never end. This "fear" became a goal and time stood still for you.

It is a natural phenomenon that happens in every day life. How could this natural phenomenon benefit you during hypnosis?

Let's say that you have a problem with self-confidence. You only have ten minutes to concentrate in hypnosis. You want to use a prescription that allows you to visualize a successful event. Assume that the experience will normally take five minutes in real time. If you tell yourself to allow the five-minute visualization to feel like two hours of experiencing the successful event, imagine the extra positive feelings you will achieve. You will boost your self-confidence once the hypnotic trance is terminated. Instead of feeling that the majority of time in your life, you have been unsuccessful, you will feel that the majority of time in your life you are very successful. This is due to the time distortion phenomenon of *time expansion*.

Clinical hypnotherapists in helping clients with "pain management," also *time expansion*. If a client has a twinge of pain every thirty seconds, a hypnotherapist, under the direction of a medical doctor, may give suggestions to the patient that the thirty-second interval is really five hours. The patient may still feel the twinges of pain; however, he will have five hours of pain free life.

Time contraction is the third feature of the time distortion, phenomena. Time contraction occurs when real-time is perhaps an hour where as hypnotic trance time is actually two minutes. Why would you use time contraction?

Again, suppose you are suffering from pain. Let's assume that the pain duration is over an hour, then you experience two hours of relief, and then you experience an hour of pain again. Using time contraction during the hypnotic condition you can contract the one-hour duration of pain to maybe ten minutes. You may then use time expansion for the two hours of relief. You may expand the time of relief from two hours to four hours. You are then able to condition the client to experiencing more life without pain.

Dissociation

Dissociation is an interesting phenomenon of hypnosis. Dissociation allows the subject or hypnotee to experience sensations as if he/she has left their own body.

Again, this is a very natural phenomenon. Think about the prisoners of war from the Viet Nam and Korean Wars. There are many accounts of a prisoners being tortured by their captors. When the torture became so painful, many times a prisoner would say that he felt his spirit lift out of this body and watch the torture take place. He would experience empathy for the body he was watching being tortured. However, he would experience no pain.

Many times, children that experience severe child abuse will have situations where their minds takes them to a different place or time as the abuse is taking place. It is the child's way of coping with the event. The hypnotherapist uses dissociation to relieve a person of physical or psychological pain.

A person may have been a witness to a horrible automobile accident where every one was killed in the automobile but him. The insurance company cannot find any witnesses that remember what events took place causing the accident. The lone survivor of the accident cannot remember anything of the accident because his subconscious mind is blocking everything that happened that day out of his conscious memory. In order to restore the memory of the survivor of the accident, dissociation may be indicated. When the survivor is hypnotized he is told to create a movie screen in his mind. Further, he is then viewing this incident from a seat in a movie theater and not participating in the events on the screen. Then he is told to recreate and watch the movie screen and view the accident. By dissociating the survivor from the accident and by taking the entire emotional trauma out of the conscious memory, the survivor has an excellent chance to recreate the accident.

Age Regression

Hypnotic age regression is one of the most interesting phenomena associated with hypnosis. When people are regressed in time, they feel that they are remembering events very clearly, that took place years ago. They may experience the same sensations of sound, sight, smell, taste and touch that they experienced in another time or they may just see events as if they are watching a movie. Usually they are not that emotionally attached.

Revivification is the actual reliving of a past event. The hypnotist actually becomes a stranger in this process. If the hypnotee or client is regressed to an age of four or five, his understanding of vocabulary and concepts will be that of a typical five or six year old. If that regressed person is to recall events that happened when he was twenty or thirty years old, he will not know what to say because he is now experiencing life as a five or six year old child. The subject or hypnotee will actually relive the event with all of emotion that was present when the event first occurred.

Age regression as it was outlined in the dissociation example of the automobile accident earlier, is more artificial. The hypnotee will know who the hypnotist is at all times and will know he is recreating the event as an adult as opposed to reliving it as a child. This is a great tool that is being used by hypnotherapists, psychologists, and psychiatrists around the world.

Hypermnesia

Hypermnesia is a fantastic effect of hypnosis! Hypermnesia is an accentuation of memory while the person is being hypnotized. Even without suggesting age regression or revivification, the hypnotee will increase his memory. Just by the process of relaxing the body, the memory will become very stimulated.

Every incident in your life has been recorded in memory. You conscious memory handles only those memories that are most recent or help you retain a certain skill you exercise often, such as driving a car or reading. With "hypermnesia," you are able to tap the vast memory included in your subconscious mind. You will be able to remember events and people you thought you forgot. This is a common "side effect" of hypnosis and your self-hypnosis session.

Hyperesthesia

Hyperesthesia refers to the increased sensitivity to all of the senses while the subject is in a hypnotic condition. If the hypnotic subject is instructed to feel heat or cold, or if he is asked to hear something that isn't there, the subject is reacting to hyperestesia.

Hyperestesia is easier to produce than anesthesia. Therefore many times a therapist will suggest hyperestesia to get the subject some success in feeling greater sensation. After the subject is successful with that, the hypnotist will suggest anesthesia for that part of the body. This technique is very effective for hypnotherapists.

Anesthesia

This is a great benefit of hypnosis and self-hypnosis.

I wonder why dentists and doctors don't use it more often. Sure, it may take the doctor or dentist up to forty minutes to hypnotize, test, and condition a patient to remove the pain from the affected part of the body. But, once that is done, the subject can be conditioned to create a profound anesthesia or analgesia, immediately. While the patient is in the waiting room, the profound anesthesia is taking effect. The patient can turn it on at will. Hypnotic anesthesia may be used again and again with absolutely no harmful side effects. There will be no drug induced hangover and in the case of a dentist, no numbing sensation in the mouth that prevents the dentist to working on both sides of the mouth during a single visit. He won't have to worry that the patient will swallow or bite off his tongue. His patient won't be squirming around in his chair because of his fear of needles either.

Hypnotic anesthesia has a much longer history than traditional drug anesthesia. I hope more medical doctors and dentists find it useful in their practices.

Harmful Effects of Hypnosis

Yes, there are some harmful effects of hypnosis. I have listed some of the harmful effects of hypnosis. I think the most important one for people to realize is that we experience the hypnotic condition, even when there is no hypnotist around. When we are children under the age of seven or eight, we are in the state of hypnosis almost all the time.

Therefore it is very important for parents to take note.

Children and Hypnosis

Children under the age of seven or eight, before the sense of

162

reason develops, are in the state of hypnosis nearly all of the time. They are hypersensitive to any and all suggestions their parents give them.

Have you ever wondered why a Mother picks up her child when the child gets a cut or a scratch? The Mother then kisses the wound. Mother says to the child, "It will be all better now because Mommy has kissed it." Guess what? The child stops crying, forgets about the wound and continues playing again.

Parents sometimes say hurtful remarks to their children. Listening to remarks that will tear down the child's self-esteem and self-confidence, the child will except those remarks and possibly go through life with low self-esteem and low self-confidence. Always give children positive and loving suggestions.

Neglect of Suggestion Removal

Sometimes a stage hypnotist, as well as a clinician will forget to remove the suggestions of the hypnotic session. That may become a problem, especially in the case of pain management.

The subject may be instructed to create anesthesia in his hand, (this is called glove anesthesia) and then rub his hand on the part of the body that needs to be anesthetized. The part of the body in the case of a dental patient may be the side of the face. However, after the session if the dentist or hypnotist doesn't remove the suggestion that the numb hand will return to its previous sensation, the person may slam his car door on his numb hand and not get proper treatment. Since the patient will not feel any pain in his hand, he may deny treatment and a serious injury may result.

Always remove the suggestions after the hypnotic session.

Workshop

Name and discuss 5 effects of hypnosis. How may each be employed in hypnotherapy?

1.

2.

3.

4.

5.

Activity 2 - More Theory

List 2 places you may find more information on hypnosis theory.
Read one article or book on hypnosis theory.

1.

2.

Activity 3 - Self-hypnosis Forum

Fire up your computer, get on the Internet and go to the Self-hypnosis Forum located at: http://www.wayneperkins.net
Read and post any questions or concerns you have regarding hypnosis theory.
Record your ideas and impressions below.

Summary

In Chapter 14, you learned some of the theory behind hypnosis. You were given some examples how this theory is applied in clinical situations. You will learn more theory by reading the books listed in the bibliography. The bibliography is located in the appendix of this book. You will also find more theory on the Hypnotism Education Website located at http://www.wayneperkins.net
Learning theory will assist you in achieving all of your goals in life.
This is the end of *How To Hypnotize Yourself Without Losing Your Mind.*
Always remember that this book, just like your life, is a work in progress. Once you send me the registration information form located in the appendix, you will have access to additional pages, chapters, and changes regarding this book. You will also

receive the free e-mail newsletter, called *The Goal Achievement Newsletter.*

You will have access to me via my website, e-mail address, and the free self-hypnosis workshop you may attend. This workshop is based on this book.

I wish you all the best in your pursuits. Always remember that you are the best hypnotist that ever existed for yourself. You will succeed!

You can hypnotize yourself...without losing your mind.

My words will go with you wherever and whenever you need them.

...And always remember.

"My mission in life is to help you achieve your mission in life."

--Wayne F. Perkins, Certified Clinical Hypnotherapist

Appendix A-1

By filling out all the information required and sending me the registration form you are entitled the following:

1. Updated versions of this on-demand-published book. You will receive new pages or even full chapters of new information.
2. Discounts on Wayne F. Perkins hypnosis workshops and seminars.
3. Free e-mail newsletter: *The Goal Achievement Newsletter.*
4. Discounts on new books, tapes, and other media created by Wayne F. Perkins.
5. FREE admission to the full-day workshop called *How to Hypnotize Yourself Without Losing Your Mind.* Discounts for your friends and relatives when they attend any of Wayne F. Perkins' workshops or seminars.
6. Discounts on any of Wayne F. Perkins' Hypnotic Age Regression, Stress Management or Sales Improvement Using Hypnosis seminars and workshops.
7. Access to the Hypnosis Bookstore, located on the Internet
8. Free access to the Self-hypnosis Forum Website on the Internet.
9. Free Access to the Self-hypnosis Chat Service Website on the Internet.

Registration Form

Please complete the following and send to the address listed below:

Name:
_____

Address:
_____

City: State:
_____

Region: Country:
_____

Phone: Email Address:

_____

Complete and send form to: Wayne F. Perkins

                               18662 North 42nd Street

                               Phoenix, AZ 85050

                               Or e-mail information to:

                               Wayne@wayneperkins.net

Appendix A-2
What Will I Gain or Lose?

Think about these questions: What will I gain by achieving this goal? What will I lose by achieving this goal?

Think about how your goal achievement will change your life.

For example, if you are trying to control your weight, you will lose fat and you may also lose friends who would rather see you in the fat state you are in. For some reason they may feel that your success in weight control diminishes them in some way. I am sure in your life experiences you have similar examples on how friends and relative really perceive you and support you in your success.

What will I gain by achieving my listed goals?

1.

2.

3.

4.

5.

What I will lose by achieving my listed goals?

1.

2.

3.

4.

5.

Appendix A-3
Induction Evaluation Form

Record your reactions and thoughts to this induction by answering the following questions.

5. What was the first thing you thought about as you finished the exercise?

6. How did you feel during the exercise?

7. How do you feel now?

8. Did you have any unusual sensations as you were listening to your voice?

9. List anything that you felt was "memorable" during the exercise.

Appendix A-4
What Are Your Goals?

Activity 1- What Are Your Goals?

List below 5 goals you wish to achieve.
1.

2.

3.

4.

5.

Activity 2 - What Will I Gain or Lose?

Think about this question: What will I gain by achieving this goal? Think about how your goal achievement will change your life. Also list all of the things you may lose as a result of your goals achievement. For example, if you are trying to control your weight, you will *lose* fat and you may also lose friends who would rather see you in the fat state you are in. For some reason they may feel that your success in weight control, someone diminishes them in some way. I am sure in your life experiences you have similar examples on how friends and relative really perceive you and support you in your success.

What will I gain by achieving my listed goals?

1.

2.

3.

4.

5.

What I will lose by achieving my listed goals?
1.

2.

3.

4.

5.

Appendix A-5
Self-hypnosis Induction 1: Eyes Open Method

Always remember that ALL hypnosis is self-hypnosis! You are always in control. You have all the power necessary to make positive changes in your own life. You may have found out already in life that you also have the power to make all the negative changes in your life. Let's focus on the positive changes.

Find an area in your home or place of work where you can have about 10 minutes to yourself. That's right, only 10 minutes are needed in your quest for a successful induction at this point. After practicing this exercise many times, you may reduce the time to only one or two minutes. Now read the following words into a recording device. Read very, very slowly. Pretend that you are tired as you read this exercise and you will react in a relaxed, sleepy, manner. You will find yourself empathetic to your own voice. You may want to print out this page for future reference. Whenever you see the (Pause) cue, pause for 3 seconds, then go ahead and read again. Let your body relax for a few moments before continuing to record.

BEGINNING OF EXERCISE

Sit up in a comfortable chair or lie on a couch or a bed with your hands resting in your lap or by your side and take three slow deep breaths. Each time you inhale, focus on filling your lungs with clean, fresh air. (Pause)

As you exhale, feel all of the tension leave your lungs. (Pause)

Now stare at a spot. Look at a spot on the wall or ceiling. (Pause)

Look at that spot, breathe deep and relax. (Pause)

Your body is relaxing, deeply relaxing. (Pause)

Your eyes are getting heavy and closing down. (Pause)

You are going deep, deep, and deeper into a pleasant state of relaxation. (Pause)

Your mind is alert and aware, and your body is relaxing, perfectly. You feel good, you feel fine...you feel perfectly relaxed. (Pause)

Each and every deep breath that you take lets you relax deeper and deeper. (Pause)

Each and every sound that you hear allows you to relax deeper and deeper. (Pause)

Nothing will disturb you. Just breathe deeply and relax deeply. (Pause)

Let your body relax. (Pause)

Let all of your muscles relax as you gain control over the powerful subconscious part of our mind. (Pause)

All of your cares and troubles are just drifting away. (Pause)

You can bring them back at any time you want. (Pause)

However, it feels good to let them drift away at this time. (Pause)

But it feels good to let them drift away at this time. Each and every breath you take allows you to relax deeper and deeper each and every sound that you hear, allows you to relax deeper and deeper. (Pause)

You feel good. You feel fine. You feel perfectly and completely relaxed. (Pause)

Your mind is alert and aware and your body

is relaxing perfectly. Now allow your eyelids to feel heavy. (Pause)

Allow your eyes to feel tired. Begin to close your eyelids down tight. This will allow you to relax deeper, deeper and sounder than ever before (Pause)

You are going down deeper and sounder in this wonderful state of relaxation. (Pause)

Your mind is keenly alert and aware, and your body is relaxing perfectly. (Pause)

Now picture in your mind that with your eyes closed down tightly, you can see out of an imaginary hole in the top of your head. (Pause)

Imagine that you are looking out of that imaginary hole or window and you can see a beautiful relaxing scene around you. (Pause)

You make be picturing the night sky, or a beautiful daytime scene with mountains and trees, or a lake or the ocean shore. Or, you may be picturing a comfortable room or place that is very quiet and still. (Pause)

Whatever picture you hold in your mind, just hold it there and relax deeply and soundly. (Pause)

Now I am going to count from three down to one. With every count take a long slow deep breath. Then exhale deeply, and allow yourself to relax deeper and sounder than ever before. (Pause)

Okay, three breathing deeply, two, inhaling deeply and exhaling. Feel the tension leaving your lungs. (Pause)

One, deeper and more completely relaxed than ever before (Pause)

· You feel relaxed, focused and at peace. (Pause)

Each time you practice this exercise, You

will find yourself relaxing to a greater and greater degree. (Pause)

Your body feels totally relaxed as your mind is keenly alert, aware and very powerful. (Pause)

You can achieve anything YOU want when you execute your own power. (Pause)

You will sleep better when its time to sleep and you will find more energy when you are awake. (Pause)

Your life is getting better and better. (Pause)

Day by day, in every way you are getting better and better. (Pause)

You feel good. You feel fine you feel totally and completely, relaxed. In a moment I am going to count from 1 to 5. (Pause)

By the time I reach 5, you will be alert and awake and feeling better than you have ever felt before. (Pause)

Each and every time you practice this exercise, you will find yourself relaxing to a greater and greater degree. (Pause)

All right, one, two, three, four, five. (Pause)

You are wide-awake, alert and feeling better in every way!

END OF EXERCISE

How do you feel? Do you feel alert and awake and feeling better than you have ever felt before?

Appendix A-6
Self-hypnosis Induction 2: Eyes Closed Method

Find a great place to sit or lie down and relax. Again, you will be talking into your voice-recording device. You will listen and then evaluate. Remember to add three seconds each time you see the word "pause" as you are recording.

Remember to use the word "you" when recording this information to yourself. You may then work with using the word "I" and substitute it for "you" later on.

BEGINNING OF INDUCTION

Get comfortable sitting in your chair or lying down on your bed or couch. As you sit in your chair or lie on the bed or couch, you are going deep, deep, and deeper into relaxation. (Pause)

You will accomplish deep relaxation today. (Pause)

Close your eyelids down tight, shutting out the light. (Pause)

As you close your eyelids down, shutting out the light, your body is relaxing deeply. (Pause)

In a moment, you are going to take three slow, deep breaths. (Pause)

Each time you inhale, draw the air in slowly and deeply. (Pause)

Each time you exhale, focus on pushing all the tension out of your lungs. (Pause)

181

As you breathe in the fresh, clean air, you feel relaxed and satisfied. (Pause)

One, inhale slowly, take a very deep breath. Hold it for a moment. (Pause)

Now exhale, (Pause) let all the tension leave your body. (Pause)

Two, inhale slowly, and as you exhale, feel the tension leaving your lungs. (Pause)

Three, inhale slowly, and as you exhale, feel all the tension leaving your body, and all of the tension, leaving your lungs. (Pause)

As you exhale, you feel all of the tension leaving your lungs and all of the tension leaving your body. (Pause).

Nothing will disturb you, just focus on your deep, peaceful, relaxation. (Pause)

Your mind is alive and alert, and your body is relaxing deeply, soundly and perfectly as if you were in a deep, sound, sleep. (Pause)

All of your muscles are letting go as you go deeper into this pleasant relaxation. (Pause)

Your mind is keenly alert and aware, as your body is relaxing perfectly. (Pause)

Each and every muscle and fiber in your body is relaxed, as you go deeper and deeper into the self-hypnotic state of mind.

Your mind is always keen and alert, and your body is relaxing deeply and soundly. (Pause)

Now that that your body is completely relaxed, your mind is focused on the suggestions I give you. (Pause)

Picture in your mind that you are looking at the night sky. (Pause)

Picture the night sky complete with stars and planets and a full moon, or you may picture the sky with no stars and planets and no moon at all. (Pause)

Whatever sky you picture in your mind will be the correct one. (Pause)

Now right in the middle of the night sky, picture a large wheel. (Pause)

It can be a wagon wheel or automobile wheel or bicycle wheel. (Pause)

Whatever wheel you picture in your mind will be the correct one. Now as you picture the wheel in your mind, imagine that the wheel is turning. (Pause)

Let it turning clockwise or counter clockwise, fast or slow. Just imagine it turning. (Pause)

As the wheel is spinning and turning, you are going deeper and deeper into the hypnotic state of mind. (Pause)

Your mind is keen and alert, as your body is relaxing perfectly. (Pause)

Each and every deep breath is allowing you to relax deeply. (Pause)

Each and every sound that you hear is allowing you to relax very deeply. (Pause)

Now begin to drop the thoughts of the night sky and the wheel. You will now prepare to emerge from this wonderful state of mind. (Pause)

In a moment I am going to count from one to five. At the count of five, you will be wide-awake and alert and feeling better than you have ever felt before. (Pause)

If you are listening to this tape just before you are going to sleep at night, you will be able to turn off the tape and go to sleep immediately. (Pause)

Waking up when you want to, feeling alive and alert and better than you have ever felt before. (Pause)

If you need to be awake after listening to this tape, you will be wide-awake and alert and feeling better than you have ever felt before. You will have energy that will last all day. (Pause)

When you go to bed later, you will be able to sleep all night and feel very rested in the morning. (Pause)

All right, one, beginning to emerge from hypnosis, two feeling better than you have ever felt before, three, four, get ready now, five, wide awake, alert, feeling great in every way. Yawn, stretch, feel good!

END OF INDUCTION

How do you feel? Wasn't that fun? I hope you enjoyed it.

Appendix B Bibliography

Aarons, Harry and Marne F. H. Bubeck M.Ed. *The Handbook of Professional Hypnosis.* Power Publishers Inc: South Orange New Jersey, 1971.

Aarons, Harry, *Hypnotic Conditioning for Childbirth.* Power Publishers, Inc: South Orange New Jersey, 1960.

Copelan, Rachel. *How to Hypnotize Yourself and Others,* Harper and Rowe: New York, 1981

Coue`, Emile, *How to Practice Suggestion and Autosuggestion.* American Library Service: New York, 1923.

Erickson, Milton H. *Advanced Techniques of Hypnosis and Therapy.* Grune & Stratton, Inc: New York,and London, 1967

Estabrooks, George H. *Hypnotism.* E.P. Dutton & Co: New York, 1957.

Gindes, Bernard, M. D., *New Concepts of Hypnosis.* Wilshire Book Company: Hollywood, 1951

Jones E. *The Action of Suggestion in Psychotherapy.* Journal of Abnormal Psychology 5, 217-254, 1910.

Kroger, William S., *Clinical and Experimental Hypnosis.* J. B. Lippincott Co: Philadelphia, 1977.

LeCron, Leslie, and Bordeaux, Jean. *Hypnotism Today,* Grune and Stratton, Inc: New York, 1947.

McGill, Ormond, *The New Encyclopedia of Stage Hypnotism.* The Anglo American Book Company LTD: Underwood,St Clears, Carmmarthen, Wales. 1996.

Spiegel, Herbert and Spiegel, David, *Trance and Treatment: Clinical Uses of Hypnosis.* Basic Books, Inc.: New York, 1978.

Appendix C-1 Menu of Services

Wayne F. Perkins offers full-day hypnosis workshops on the following topics.

1. *How To Hypnotize Yourself Without Losing Your Mind.* This is a full-day workshop where you learn how to hypnotize yourself and then use self-hypnosis and powerful goal achievement techniques to achieve your personal goals. The workshop is based on the Wayne's Self-hypnosis Training Book.

2. *Have I Lived Before?* A full-day workshop where Wayne F. Perkins, Certified Clinical Hypnotherapist, uses Hypnotic Past Life Regression to explore the possibilities of you living a previous life. Each attendee will be conditioned for a deep state of hypnosis and will be able to record his/her past life adventure on audiotape.

3. *How to Hypnotize Your Prospect Without Them Knowing It.* Another full-day workshop presented by Wayne F. Perkins, designed for sales professionals and small business owners. Attendees learn to communicate with customers and prospects using sound hypnotic techniques. This workshop improves your odds in completing the sale. Hypnosis exercises in overcoming the fear of failure and negative thoughts are also practiced and learned by each attendee.

For further information on the above Hypnosis Workshops, please contact Wayne Perkins directly.

Wayne F. Perkins   Phone: (602) 787-9195
Certified Clinical Hypnotherapist   FAX: (602) 971-6967
18662 N. 42nd St. Phoenix, AZ 85080
E-mail: wayne@wayneperkins.net

Appendix C-2
Hypnotism High School Assembly Programs! Your Most Memorable School Assembly Program!

Concert Of Mental Magic

This exciting audience participation demonstration conducted by Wayne Perkins will have students and faculty talking about it for years.

Wayne, who is a professional stage hypnotist from Phoenix, Arizona, is again presenting his *exciting audience participation shows* specifically designed for *school assembly programs.* Wayne will demonstrate amazing psychological phenomena using advanced hypnotic techniques. All hypnotic demonstrations are genuine, using volunteers from your audience.

Stimulate your creativity as you experience the true mental magic of the mind.... Hypnotism.

Hypnosis will be thrilling. Exciting mind magic will linger in the classroom long after the performance. Volunteers utilize newly acquired techniques in memory and recall as a result of their brief experience on stage.

Additional Programs For Your School!

Do you want your athletes to improve their skills? Would you like to see your band members improve their performance? Do your teachers and staff need a "mental vacation" to overcome daily stress?

In addition to the stage hypnosis performance, Wayne can

provide additional services while on your campus!
Fund raising activities for sports and band boosters and self-improvement seminars and workshops for your community can be provided. Please call now for cost and availability for an exciting school assembly experience.
Postal Mailing Address:

Wayne F. Perkins
Creative Hypnotist   Phone: 602.787.9195
18662 N. 42nd St.   FAX: 602.971.6967
Phoenix, AZ 85080   E-mail:school@wayneperkins.net

I look forward to working with you in making this program an exciting event and a huge success!
"My mission in life is to help you achieve your mission in life."--Wayne F. Perkins

Appendix C-3 About the Author

Wayne F. Perkins, is a Certified Clinical Hypnotherapist and Stage Hypnotist who resides in Phoenix, Arizona.

Wayne presents his *How to Hypnotize Yourself Without Losing Your Mind,* public workshops and to business groups and associations throughout the country.

Along with teaching Self-hypnosis Wayne presents workshops on Hypnotic Past Life Regression and Stress Management. He has personally developed techniques in Pain Management, and has worked with people suffering from life threatening illnesses. Wayne has developed exercises to stimulate the immune system that are located on the Hypnotism Website at:

http://www.wayneperkins.net

In addition Wayne F. Perkins has presented his *Concert of Stage Hypnotism,* to high schools and colleges for over 20 years. In his demonstrations he uses all volunteers from the audience. Wayne entertains and helps students overcome test anxiety.

Wayne also gives sales training to companies and teaches sales professionals how to hypnotize their clients as well as how to apply powerful goal achievement skills and self-hypnosis with professional selling. Wayne has over 16 years as a successful sales professional and sales trainer.

Wayne F. Perkins, is Certified by the American Board of Hypnotherapy and received his training at the American Institute of Hypnotherapy, and the Hypnotism Institute of Chicago.

Wayne taught Business Education at Elgin High School in Elgin, Illinois from 1972-1975. He received his Bachelor of Science in Business Education from Northern Illinois University in DeKalb, Illinois. He taught *Self-hypnosis for Self-*

improvement at Triton College in River Grove, Illinois.
You can find more information about and pictures of Wayne at his website at:

http://www.wayneperkins.net

Appendix D-1 Internet Health Care Websites

One good reason for getting access to the Internet is all of the free information available concerning maintaining good health. The following are free resources available to you as you surf the Internet:

Achoo:

This site connects you to thousands of health-related sites and news groups. The site location is: http://www.achoo.com

GriefNef:

A variety of resources related to death and dying are provided here. Includes poetry, bulletin boards and support groups. The website location is: http://rivendell.org

HypnoDirect.com

This site provides a directory of hypnotherapist from around the world. Links to helpful hypnosis sites are included. Site address is: http://www.hypnodirect.com

Hypnosis.Com:

Free hypnosis scripts and information on NLP is provided by the American Board of Hypnotherapy. Certification programs are available here. The site location is: http://hypnosis.com

Hypnotism Education:

Created by Wayne F. Perkins, Certified Clinical Hypnotherapist, this site includes free hypnosis scripts and the largest Hypnosis Bookstore on the Internet. The website is located at: http://www.wayneperkins.net

Appendix D-2 Internet Health Care Websites

National Breast Cancer Coalition:

This is an action and advocacy group determined to eradicate breast cancer. The website address is: http://www.natlbcc.org

National Health Information Center:

This is a health referral service that puts consumers and health professionals in touch with each other. The site location is: http://www.nhic-nt.health.org

National Hospice Organization:

Serving the need of people facing life challenging illnesses and their families is the purpose of this site. It is located at: http://www.nho.org

Sleep Medicine Home Page:

This site includes newsgroups, discussion groups, and professional associations focussing on sleep disorders. The site location is: http://www.cloud9.net/~thorpy

SleepNet:

SleepNet provides information on sleep disorders. It includes hyperlinks to sleep centers and support groups. It is located at: http://www.sleepnet.com

The HIV InfoWeb:

This page provides information about HIV and AIDS treatments and related issues. The website is located at: http://www.infoweb.org